Hockey Sucks
Let's Fix It

Michael Munro

Blue Swell Books
Nanaimo, B.C.
Canada

First Print Edition: October 2017
ISBN: 978-1-988257-15-0

THOU who stealest fire,
From the fountains of the past,
To glorify the present, oh, haste,
Visit my low desire!
Strengthen me, enlighten me!
I faint in this obscurity,
Thou dewy dawn of memory.

- Lord Alfred Tennyson

CONTENTS

INTRODUCTION

The following is an essay regarding the current state of the NHL from a journalist and fan's perspective. I covered the NHL in the late 1980s and early 1990s from Vancouver and was lucky to meet and interview stars from Eric Lindros to Trevor Linden to Igor Larionov and Gino Odjick and to listen to GMs such as Pat Quinn, Brian Burke and George McPhee. It was a real privilege to be around the NHL and I have nothing but the highest regards for all of those involved in the game and the incredible athletic ability and intelligence of these men and women. Like any journalist I was able to look briefly behind the scenes but I did not play in the NHL and so this is mostly a third person perspective.

I trained as a journalist and the highest level of hockey I played was college. My dad died when he was just 41 (cancer) and I was 16 and my NHL dream, however farfetched, died with him. My older brother and a great bunch of loggers, the Port McNeill Goodtimers, got me on their team where I got beer, parties and a lifeline. So my love of hockey is perhaps a little more personal for me than you. And whatever road I was going to travel beforehand it included hockey afterwards. Hockey binds most Canadian families even those who have left.

I hope this article begins a frank discussion of the NHL's entertainment value or lack thereof. This started while talking to my brothers about the state of the game.

"Hey. You watching the game tonight?"

"I haven't watched in years."

And then I realized I haven't watched one in years either. And by that I mean sitting down from beginning to end and really paying attention. And not just to the local team but to any game at any time.

"Why?"

"It's unwatchable."

And they're right. There's no 50 goal scorers. The Art Ross Trophy winner barely scratches 100 points and 30 goals. There's no fights. There's no hits. And the game resembles Red Rover and takes as long as a cricket game. It's hard to stomach.

To be fair, time has passed since I first fell in love with hockey. The further you get from the time you first held a stick the further the emotion dissipates. Youth adds romance to life in everything.

And so before memory and passion fail me I thought I should write this to no one in particular but with the hope it finds someone who can pick up this torch and carry it further. It's more than a game to Canada and has become a part of the vibrant fabric of America over the centuries. It is the bond between fathers and mothers, sons and daughters. It is a shared memory of nations tying past to future. It is history and worth saving because Canada and America represent all that is best in the world. And the more hockey changes the less those ties bind.

Usually one carries on the pursuit of hockey through their sons or daughters but I was blessed in a different way that allows a unique perspective. My daughter is pursuing academics and my son is a pursuit all on his own. He has special needs and so our path together has strayed way off the beaten course and for this I am very grateful. It allowed me to view the NHL from outside of its pursuits by parents and to observe them rather than participate. It's very difficult to be objective about something when you're fully engaged in it. I am most definitely not.

I was in a tent at a Cub Scouts field trip, no more than six or seven, with my brother on the Queen Charlotte Islands (now Haida Gwaii), when the pack leader ran to the circle of tents and yelled "Bobby Orr scored! He scored! Canada won!" This was my introduction to professional hockey. I had no idea what Canada had won in 1976 nor what Canada was or who Bobby Orr was. We had been given penknives for the trip and nothing else mattered. Why would it?

There was no television to speak of really in my first hometown where I played road hockey all day. From time to time the CBC would come in on my parent's black and white television when the rabbit ears were adjusted just right on Saturdays. Through the static I could see Guy Lafleur of this Montreal Canadiens team. I had no idea where Montreal was but Guy was my guy. It never occurred to me Montreal wore red, white and blue, they were of course black and white. And that was the extent of the NHL in my life.

Everyday after school there was a road hockey game. And I played 2-3 hours each and every day in front of our house from the age of three. I never saw ice until I was seven or eight years old (the Queen Charlotte Islands are mostly immune to that Canadian disease called snow and ice.) When the pond at the end of Tingley Street, Port Clements, froze one day the volunteer fire department made up of young loggers, who must have left work early, came to the end of the street with an old red fire truck and white water tank and hose and sprayed the ice for us bewildered children. I don't know where my dad found skates for me and my brother but he did, old leather skates with long steel blades and white knobs on the end. I had no idea what they were. (You can't see what hockey players wear on an old black and white television with much static.)

When dad took us to the pond, I stared at him when he suggested I try to stand on the ice wearing these metal things. I think my brother was braver and ventured out, one wobbly ankle at a time, and I followed.

My bullbucking dad moved us to Port McNeill when I was 10. There was an arena and ice and I hated to leave it every day following. I lived at public skating and went to every single one I could. I used to get on my hands and knees and run my palm along the ice and feel its strange tingly grasp upon it. I still do that outside on a frozen puddle or car hood when winter comes, if it comes.

Before this time games were conversations on the road between homework with the same friends. After this time we wore skates, pads, and I got gloves and a shiny new wooden stick and a dressing room with people wearing the same sweater. We were an army preparing for battle. I still miss the butterflies you get before a game; the memory stays with me all these decades later. Nothing ever replaces the sting of the cold air when entering an arena or joining your teammates chattering with excitement. I got really good really quickly because I had thousands of hours playing hockey and skating just completed it for me. The only passion I had for anything was hockey. And then life happened, as it does to everyone, perhaps me a little sooner than others, and you look back and it's 30 years passed in the blink of an eye.

Canada doesn't produce great hockey players anymore.

We don't provide the toppings for the meal we provide the meat and potatoes.

It's unacceptable because when Canada stops providing talent then the NHL is worse off. Just like you I want to see someone score 50 goals in 50 games again. But there's nobody currently in the game or coming in the game or possibly even born today who can provide

the Maurice Richard magic. Mike Bossy, Wayne Gretzky, Mario Lemieux, Brett Hull, Jarri Kurri, Alexander Mogilny and Cam Neely are all members of that exclusive club and they all have something in common. They all grew up at the same time. They're virtually the same age (Richard exempt of course) and there's been nothing since then.

I ask the simple question: why did it stop?

I must state upfront I fully expect disagreement with my arguments. They would not be arguments were it not for this. I don't have all the answers. I have some questions and some observations. I hope I have put these in conversational format as if you and I were sitting at a bar and having a few beers and I lay out my thoughts. I hope you will take pen and paper after being kind enough to read these arguments and to respond accordingly in whichever format you see fit.

I prefer the modern form of books (and I offer a heartfelt Canadian apology to those I have offended) for I live amongst the wood used for paper and I know the paper is better used for something other than my essay. It also allows me to quickly update this should I remember something in the future. So I hope you take the time to read to the end because it's better than the beginning, or so it appears to me, that every argument is always better at the end. And I hope it is a statement to those in Canadian hockey who proclaim "oh, everything is fine" when it's obviously not.

I start with the premise that the NHL in its current format is a far cry from its heyday. You may disagree summarily with that preface and I fully understand. My time has passed and perhaps you see things from your mountain top which I cannot find on the atlas no matter how hard I peer because time is like that. Albert Einstein says time after all is not a straight line but is defined in ever moving peaks and valleys and I'm at the bottom and can't see your vantage point anymore. I used to follow the game religiously. I suppose it was a way of keeping my father alive. And also it helped to pass some very mundane valleys of tedious jobs to run these statistics in my head. I would know the height and weight and draft position of every player in the league. But that's faded away with my disinterest of the game. And so I thought it's time to write these things down before I couldn't care less about the National Hockey League or hockey in general.

These arguments are supportive and can't be taken alone to try to define why it stopped. It's not as simple as saying goalie gear. Once you start exploring the why behind the issue it quickly expands. But I think it's worth looking. In this book I mention some people such as Patrick Roy and Jacques Lemaire and it is not my intention to demean them in anyway. Quite the contrary. They were brilliant players and Lemaire an even better coach. They had to have been great to make such monumental impact on an entire society. And almost everyone who has played for them or with them has said they were spectacular. I don't point the blame at anyone. I don't think this problem was created by anyone with ill-intent. Quite the opposite in fact.

Most of these people I mention are Canadian and with that comes a sense of politeness and respect. And for all his detractors, NHL Commissioner Gary Bettman has been terrific for the game of hockey. Yes, he's a little awkward in front of a camera but I don't think he ever did anything with the intention of bad results. It's his business to provide entertainment. I think everyone who has ever been involved with the game has seen the fans in the buildings and felt some degree of wanting to provide entertainment. Of course they did, there's people staring at them from seats who paid money to see them.

I think it's like tuning up your 1992 chevy 350. You try to make it perform better by adding hotter plugs, and K&N filters, and synthetic oil, and performance ignitions, and higher octane gas, and performance wires until you realize, several hundred dollars later, you wasted your time. You'll only ever get 176 horsepower out of the old girl and her carbureted fuel injection (yes that was a thing) and it's best to just leave it original as engineers designed. It can't be upgraded and was never meant to be upgraded. It's running as intended.

WHERE'S THE TALENT?

In 2016, the Pittsburgh Penguins won the Stanley Cup in games of Red Rover Red Rover we call San Jose Sharks center Joe Thornton over. The games didn't showcase skill. In fact the person who won the Conn Smythe trophy as the tournament's best player (as voted on by the media and we'll get to that problem) didn't score a goal in the Finals, was a collective -4 in the playoffs and didn't scrub a point per game in the postseason.

In 2017 Pittsburgh duplicated the feat literally with a bunch of guys on the blue line proving winning the Stanley Cup had nothing to do with talent anymore. Hockey has hit rockbottom and it's time to say it. There's hardly anything distinguishable from the best players in the game to the worst player. Wayne Gretzky scored 47 points in 18 playoff games in 1985 including 16 goals in 18 games. Crosby scored six goals in 24 games in 2016. It's about 30 percent of Gretzky's production.

So what happened? How did it fall apart from such a magical game to something resembling speed skating? Where did the hockey go? In the following pages I hope to begin an honest discussion of possible causes and I follow these arguments with some solutions. The NHL didn't get here deliberately. Every move they made was designed to help the game with really good intentions. And for short periods of time it worked. But the culmination of all the efforts has led to a game which is hard to watch. I mean you really have to be committed to watch an NHL game especially an NHL playoff game. There's tons of skating back and forth and virtually no action taking place on the ice. Scoring a goal in the NHL is no longer art it is laborious. And the games are too long.

In 1994, the best Stanley Cup Finals of all time were played. They scored 40 goals in seven games. It featured two teams who went after it - the New York Rangers and the Vancouver Canucks. The Rangers' Brian Leetch pushed the play ever forward with lightning speed, throwing haymaker after haymaker at the Canucks. And the Canucks responded with the fastest player to ever play the game. The breathtaking Pavel Bure darted in and out of the Rangers defense at will throwing massive haymakers of his own.

It came down to the last shot when Nathan Lafeyette hit the post on a breakaway and the Rangers and Mark Messier carried the Cup high while a shattered and bloodied Trevor Linden collapsed to one knee watching the celebrations. The hockey was mesmerizing. Even the vaunted Sports Illustrated magazine (when magazines existed) predicted hockey was on the rise. Americans and Canadians were captivated from coast to coast to coast. It was the game at its very finest. Two championship teams equal to the task going toe-to-toe in the season's grand finale. What a series! What a game! Hundreds of thousands of people in New York celebrating in the streets and thousands of people in Vancouver rioting in excruciating emotion of the loss. It was the game played by Masters until the bitter end. A crescendo of a symphony worthy of Wolfgang Amadeus Mozart. The games had it all with hits, fights, dekes, passes, speed, power, size, blood, sweat and real tears.

It ended on June 14, 1994. Three days later the Rangers were enjoying a ticker tape parade through the city when O.J. Simpson got in a white Ford Bronco with his best friend driving holding a gun to himself and all caught live on television. At 9:37 pm Simpson surrendered to the police. All of the media attention the NHL had received for its beautiful championship culminating with a New York win melted away on a Hollywood freeway.

There's never been any series like it since. And it continued to get worse year after year until you had a Pittsburgh team win a Stanley Cup almost without goals, blood, fights, emotion or talent in 2017. It was a whimper of a series. There wasn't anything on display that you couldn't see at a local pickup game at your nearest arena. Nothing you saw done on the ice couldn't be replicated in a beer league game, albeit at a slower pace. I know many of you are saying, "Oh my God, Sidney Crosby was there!" Yes, he was in the Finals but you had to look closely to find him. It was a stinker with nary a close game. If you're honest, you'll admit none of the games showed off anything spectacular on the ice.

Crosby is without doubt the most accomplished hockey plumber in the history of the game. He does everything precisely as it should be done and not a step further. There's no magic in his game. There's nothing that drops jaws or wows anyone. He's just a really good robotic plumber out there and he epitomizes what's wrong with the game today. And what's wrong is manufactured hockey players.

The 2017 NHL Finals were a track meet and nothing more. Dump it in, chase it out, dump it in again. There was no Mario! "Oh My God - did I just see that?" as he cheekily stick-handled the puck in between Minnesota North Star defenders Neil Wilkinson and Shawn Chambers before deking a bewildered Jon Casey in goal. Who could forget the two minute standing ovation afterwards? Or on May 26, 1992, when killing a penalty,

Mario intercepted a pass out of the air, turned up ice then stick handled the puck repeatedly between the retreating Boston Bruin Raymond Bourque's feet then passing him on the left when Bourque looked right and finally deking a bewildered Andy Moog. That was Penguin magic.

It's hard to remember if Crosby played the playoff games in 2016 or 2017 at all he was that invisible with his six and eight goals in those playoff runs respectively. And in fact the former Toronto Maple Leafs star Phil Kessel, an American, foolishly traded by Toronto to Pittsburgh in 2015, led Pittsburgh to the Stanley Cup in both points and goals with 10 goals and 22 points in 2016 compared to Crosby's six goals, 19 points and -4 (he was on the ice four more times when the opposition scored than when his team scored.) And in 2017 Kessel bettered Crosby again. In fact it was Russian Evgeni Malkin in 2017 with his 10 goals and 28 points who led the Penguins to the Cup and not Crosby. An American and a Russian clearly outplayed Canada's Crosby in all aspects of the game yet stunningly they did not win the NHL's most valuable player award for the playoffs called the Conn Smythe.

Later in this book we'll explore the absurdity of the Conn Smythe voting where the majority of the voters are from the Toronto area. If you thought the Toronto media were going to accept anyone but Crosby as the Conn Smythe winner you're sadly mistaken. They were, after all, part of the reason Kessel was traded out of Toronto and voting for Kessel as the Conn Smythe winner would have been admitting they knew nothing about hockey.

I don't want this to sound like an anti-Crosby rant though. Crosby had his moments in the playoffs in both years. What Crosby represents though is a last gasp of Canadian hopes where media can point to a Canadian and say, see? We still produce the best hockey players when it's as plain as day Canada does not produce the best anymore. Crosby is an efficient predictable robotically trained hockey player. He's an artificial "great one." He's not the real thing. (Some of you may point to Edmonton Oilers' Connor McDavid from the Toronto area who finished 25th in the NHL goal race as the next Canadian great. I'm sorry, but almost every team in the NHL had someone with more goals than McDavid. I'm not so easily swayed by Toronto media hype. Goals matter.)

In 2016 there was no Brian Leetch controlling entire games and passing to Mark Messier at the side of the net leaving even Canuck fans to marvel at his never-ending talent and politely clapping in recognition in 1994. No, it was just simply a track meet between the Penguins and Sharks going as fast as they could up and down the ice and not stopping to try anything dangerous. And then a repeat with the Nashville Predators in 2017. Get it deep - chase after it - around and around again we go. And hockey never developed. We never saw anything magical happen during either Finals series. There was no payoff for the months of watching the season. It was just, ho-hum, I guess it's over.

Anyone can be taught to skate really fast, to dump the puck in, chase after it, make a pass to the front of the net and hope after the 30th whack at the puck something good happens. But that's not hockey. Not as we know it or love it. So what happened? How did it become unwatchable? How did it fall to the cellar floor so quickly? I'll pose the questions and my answers as to why things are the way they are now. Some of it is hockey based and a lot of it is societal. Hockey is a mere reflection of the people who play the game and the countries that supply the players. These are not robots on ice. They have a story, a history, a family behind them. And all of that contributes to what you see on the ice or in any sport we watch today. But hockey is, more than any other sport, susceptible to these societal changes. It is a game, the only game, where you play offense and defense with a physical element that requires courage. And that formula means you get out of the game what you put in. The Finals product is not a product produced in a laboratory but yet now it is played as such. How did it get to this? And just a warning, I bring a western perspective to hockey and those in the east may not like what I have to say. You have been warned. It's not done out of malice. It's my opinion from my view over here and it's one that needs to be voiced.

GOALTENDING

Montreal Canadiens goaltender Patrick Roy pretty much ruined hockey. Don't get me wrong he was a spectacular goaltender and I think the best who's ever played. And he did absolutely nothing wrong other than fundamentally change the game of hockey. He was a competitive take-no-prisoners hockey player with a French passion we love and adore. But before Roy there were goaltenders. After Roy there were positional players in net who used every gap in the rule book to make themselves better as they should have done. If you look at Roy's save percentage he starts out with .875 in 1985 and finishes at .920 in 2002. There's no other player in hockey or in any other sport who got that good over that period of time. His playoff statistics are off the chart good culminating with a .934 save % and a GAA of 1.70 in 2000/01.

It wasn't his size that was a huge advantage. Roy was slightly bigger than the goaltenders in the 1994 Finals. Canucks' Kirk McLean was 6'0" and 182 pounds and Ranger Mike Richter was 5'11" and 185 pounds. McLean was the classic standup goaltender and Richter was the active little crease minder. McLean would stack the pads and Richter would flop around hunting for that puck. Both were extremely effective but both had GAA in the 2.50 area and their teams gave up close to 230 goals in the regular season while scoring close to 300.

Offense was a key to both teams. The Rangers and Canucks were good balanced hockey teams. Both teams built towards the Finals in the steady predictable pace of young superstars and veterans moving forward built through the draft, trades and free agency. New York won the President's Trophy for best regular season record and the Canucks were coming off back-to-back franchise record seasons. The goalies were a part of it but not all of it.

Roy moved goaltending from behind the team to the front with a new style of goaltending. Not right away. Old school goaltending still existed in Dominik Hasek who won two Hart Trophies (league MVP) and six Vezinas (league best goalie) while Roy was playing. But it started to change. In 1986 Roy backstopped a terrifically balanced Montreal Canadiens to a Stanley Cup with a sparkling .923 save percentage and a 1.92 goals against average. In 1993 Roy brushed Hasek aside by single-handedly winning the Canadiens the Cup with a shocking 10 overtime victories and a less than spectacular team up front. He had a save percentage of . 930 and a GAA of 2.13. The new style of goaltender had arrived. Everyone wanted a Patrick Roy in net.

Canucks goaltender McLean was the last of the positional standup goaltenders. Canadiens goalie Roy was the butterfly inventor. Drop down on every shot with gloves up, pads down, legs split, shirt puffed outwards like a butterfly flapping its wings. He was spectacular at it. But he didn't stop there. Roy started to move the meter in terms of goaltending equipment. He invented the cheater which is a piece of equipment above the glove that made the glove bigger. And the goaltending pads started to get bigger and bigger. Before then, normal size goaltending pads would have exposed the five hole (between the legs) as the thighs on the hockey pants would touch before the pads could completely close as they lay flat on the ice. That started to disappear. Shoulder pads began to increase in size with alarming quickness, some of them even using lacrosse shoulder pads that pointed upwards at the top of the shoulder to block more of the net. They began wearing extra large shirts and pants. They no longer resembled anything like McLean or Richter.

Now I think we all know the story of this. Gear got bigger, goals became harder to get as the net appeared smaller and smaller to the shooter as he faced ever larger goalies playing the butterfly just like Roy. NHL Commissioner Gary Bettman should have stopped the growing size of the gear immediately but in his defense, goaltenders said they needed the extra protection to prevent injury. The equipment modifications happened so fast the NHL regulations fell behind.

Playing goaltender in the early NHL was crazy. They were often injured and many would throw up before a game. It wasn't until the 1960s that they started to actually wear masks. And so with that still fresh in everyone's mind, it seemed logical that goaltenders should be better protected. Goalies got hurt on shots often. Frequently teams would be down to a second and third goaltender in a season with the obvious advantages this gave world class shooters. Goaltenders were absolutely nuts and incredibly athletic at the same time. Bullfighter would be a direct comparison. Standing there with a red flag taunting the bull forward to charge and ducking away at the last moment. But that machismo died off as positional play of the goaltender became the norm. The key of this type of Roy's positional goaltending is to let the puck hit them.

The goaltender was a premiere position before Roy changed the game. People paid money to see the goaltender whether it was Grant Fuhr of the Edmonton Oilers shutting the door in the third period or Eddie Belfour of the Chicago Blackhawks and his theatrics with the puck both passing and glove hand. They were selling features of the NHL. They were crown jewels such as King Richard Brodeur of the Vancouver Canucks who for six weeks in the spring of 1982 stood on his head before Mike Bossy arrived. But Brodeur's magic disappeared the next year. Everyone wanted a goalie like Roy who was brilliant in the regular season and playoffs on a consistent basis. Roy captured no magic, he was no flash in the pan.

Positional play of the goaltender means getting the maximum amount of pads between the shooter and the net. It isn't about stopping the puck anymore with a flair like King Richard. It's about blocking and flopping. It is a system that developed more than any other position in any sport to the point that you can plug almost any goalie in and win. In the past five years of the NHL we've seen the terrible practice of next goalie up. We just saw it in Pittsburgh in 2017 when they used two goalies to win the Stanley Cup, one little different from the other. They are interchangeable and nameless. Where their talents used to rely on reflexes and reading the shooter, they now lay in playing a system. Great goalies used to be great for many years because they were immensely talented. And that never changed from year to year. Whether it was a Billy Smith of the New York Islanders or a Dominik Hasek of the Buffalo Sabres they drew crowds.

The entertainment part of the goaltender used to be a part of the package of an NHL team. But it had better not be a part of the package now. Play the position on the puck each and every time. There's very little difference from one team's goalie to another. They're all 6'5" or taller with goaltending pads from their toes to their cups. They may or may not be able to catch with their glove hand. Wicked glove speed used to be a prime feature of every goalie. Not anymore. They'd show you the net above the glove teasing you to take a shot there and - snap- the leather would flash and they'd bring the captured puck all around the world and slap it on the ice while doing the splits. It was outstanding entertainment this showboating worth the price of admission. Little guys with all kinds of courage and talent snapping miracles out of thin air.

But then Roy happened. He had all of the previous goalies talents and he was damned smart. Little by little he pushed the boundaries. Other goalies immediately followed suit. And the pads got bigger. And bigger. Until somewhere in the last decade and a half the theatrics stopped and the net became blasé. Goaltenders used to catch the puck, drop it, snap a pinpoint pass 60 feet up the ice to a forward and away they went. You don't see that anymore. Goaltenders are instructed to stop the play each and every time. Not only are the goaltenders bigger than ever before, they no longer play a part in the offensive game.

In the 1980s, it wasn't uncommon to see a goaltender catch the puck, drop it, skate 15 or 20 feet with it and fire a bomb like a quarterback in the NFL. You don't see it anymore. The gear got bigger and the goalies drop to their knees on every shot and now it's virtually impossible to start the offense from the goaltender.

Philadelphia Flyer's goaltender Ron Hextall was not only a terrific fighter but an amazing passer. So was fellow Flyer Sean Burke. You wouldn't believe it by looking at goaltenders today but back then it wasn't uncommon for them to assist on goals. Hextall accumulated 33 points and 584 penalty minutes in 13 years in the NHL. Now that is entertainment. At times the Vancouver Canucks were outscored by the Edmonton Oiler's goalie Grant Fuhr on the night. And then the Canucks got their own passer in Kirk McLean who could thread the needle with the best of them.

But if you butterfly down to your knees on every single shot like a Patrick Roy then you can't get out to stop the puck and pass it up and besides it's not part of the system anymore. Now to be fair to Roy he could pass too. He simply started the ball rolling forward on the gear getting bigger and the goalies getting bigger and the butterfly development. Now low risk is the key to a goalie's future. Don't take chances. Play it safe. Play the angles. Let the equipment do the job. Play the percentages not the hunches.

And so from year to year with every goalie playing exactly the same way there is nobody at the top. Eight different goalies have won the last 10 Vezina Trophies. The hot goalie changes from year to year, period to period. It's almost random. Montreal Canadiens' Carey Price was supposed to be the next great goaltender but of course it never materialized because every time he got to the playoffs Price met a goaltender who was better able to improvise than he was or was simply hotter at that time. Originality was completely eliminated from his game and everyone else's. Originality has risk. You can fall flat on your face. But it has amazing rewards because you can get red hot, white hot. Since no goaltender in today's game gets on top and stays on top we can surmise that there isn't a real bonafide Hall of Fame goaltender in the game today. There's a distinct possibility we've seen the last goaltender put into the Hockey Hall of Fame because they all come from the same cookie cutter.

When Toronto Maple Leafs head coach Mike Babcock coached the Men's Canadian Olympic hockey team in 2014, he preferred the unproven Carey Price over the 2010 gold medal winner Roberto Luongo. Even in those four years you saw a coach shy away from a proven gold medal winner, who played the butterfly, to go with Price from Montreal, who also played the butterfly. Now coaches were starting to pick apart the play of their proven winners for a flavour of the month who had a marginally better save percentage. The tradition of going with the veteran who had produced was thrown out the window to get a fraction of a save percentage better from a guy who had won absolutely nothing.

New Jersey Devils' Martin Brodeur was the last consistent goalie in the NHL and he's almost as important as Patrick Roy in changing the game of hockey. Brodeur was a product of a system of hockey called the Trap which I will get to in a later chapter. Brodeur was the tip of the spear when it came to cookie cutter goaltenders. Some may argue he was different because he preferred his forwards and defensemen not to block shots and allow him the view of the shots but in my books he was nothing but a butterfly goaltender playing the percentages based on a system of play Roy invented.

Brodeur furthered the process of goaltending decay by becoming a part of a system and not a system unto himself. Brodeur's success spawned goaltending coaches, clinics and media experts. All of a sudden goaltending became the thing in the NHL and everyone needed a full-time goalie coach and goalie mouthpieces multiplied like bunnies in the media. It's ironic because Brodeur really is a nameless goaltender if you think about it. He didn't do anything groundbreaking. He was a goaltender who simply played angles and let the puck come to him according to a defensive system. He was bland. He was good under pressure and utterly predictable on every play. He perfected boring to a fine art. There was no real weakness in his game when playing in that system especially with NHL great Scott Neidermeyer babysitting him. And there's been others who have followed in his footsteps such as Jonathon Quick of the Los Angeles Kings in 2012. He was also a product of a system as well as being talented.

The Devils and the 2012 Los Angeles Kings based their defensive play on angles and percentages and low risks. It was the defensive and offensive strategy rolled into one cohesive unit. Really great goaltenders such as Grant Fuhr were often left alone verses two oncoming forwards and he often won the battle. The Edmonton Oilers trusted their man to stop the puck when it really mattered and the chips were on the table. You don't see any team do that anymore and goaltending has a lot to do with it because it's virtually impossible to outscore your opponent. Only four teams had a GAA above 3.00 in 2016/17 season. The last placed Colorado Avalanche were only 1 GAA behind the league leading Washington Capitals.

If you get behind a goal in today's game, oh boy, you're in a lot of trouble. A one goal deficit isn't easily overcome in the NHL. And coaches like the safe play each and every time out for that reason. If your goalie takes risks and by extension your team play takes offensive risks to provide entertainment when the other team waits for you to make a mistake, then you're not going to last too long as a coach because you'll lose. It has been a goalie arms race since Roy arrived. It's much easier to coach a defensive strategy around a big goalie than otherwise. Goalies got bigger and their gear got bigger and the athleticism stopped shining through. And that kind of makes sense. Bigger men are usually slower than smaller men and we know that because of boxing where you can definitively say that featherweights are faster punchers than heavyweights (Mohammad Ali exempted of course.)

Heavyweight boxers got so big it moved out of the public's eye. The fate of boxing is something hockey executives should worry about. Now of course boxing also had the problem of moving to exclusive deals on PayPerView and of governing bodies who couldn't communicate and operate with each other to provide steady streams of successors. While the featherweight division continued to be a source of immense entertainment it's the heavyweights we all pay to watch. The recently deposed heavyweight champion Wladimir Klitschko is around 260 pounds. Boxing slid down in interest level in North America under his reign. Hockey is moving in the Klitschko direction with giant goalies.

They're all the same size doing exactly the same thing every night in every net in the same system. There's virtually no difference from team to team. They're all 6'5" or bigger. And the goaltending pads got bigger. And the amount of goals went down. A bigger goalie means more pad on the ice. They can pretty much spread the pads from post to post along the ice. A 6'6" NHL goalie stands 6'9" tall on his skates to the top of his helmet. They dwarf National Basketball Association and some National Football League players. And now NHL teams have started to play 6'7" goalies. Where does it stop?

In order for offense to exist, coaches must be confident they can score themselves out of a deficit. Unfortunately, that's almost impossible. In 2015/16 season every team that scored first was above .500 in the NHL. The Washington Capitals won 90 percent of their games when scoring first and the Vancouver Canucks were last at exactly .500. In 1993 the NHL league average GAA was 3.53 and the average save percentage was .885. In 2016 it was 2.51 and .915.

Goalies are dominating the NHL. The first goal in a game is critical now. And so teams became super careful about getting behind a goal. Teams become ever more cautious with the puck. Dump it in, bump and grind, get it to the front of the net bring five men back and don't turn it over! Oh my God don't turn it over at the opponent's blue line! It's this hyper attention to not turning the puck over at the blue line which is contributing to a lack of offense.

Every single great player in the NHL from Nels Stewart to Eric Lindros has made their livings at the opponent's blue line where they have the advantage over the defender. It's here that every option is open to the forward. He can dump it in, which turns the defender. He can fake dumping it in and either turn outside or inside. He can stop immediately inside the blue line. He can turn inside the blue line and dish it off in a Wayne Gretzky button hook. The variables are only limited by imagination at that one point on the ice surface with the majority of the offensive zone in front of and not behind the player with the puck.

Mario Lemieux would stand outside the blue line while dangling the puck inside. It was masterful. The defender didn't know whether Lemieux was coming or going. Russian Igor Larionov on many occasions would simply turn back to his own zone and start again, and then get to the blue line, not see what he likes, turn around and do it again. And yes, if you're of a certain age you won't have seen that, but it did happen. Paul Coffey of the Edmonton Oilers made a living doing this as a defenseman. For the true masters of the game, blue lines are their office. But there is some risk involved at the blue line. From time to time even Gretzky would turn it over at the blue line. And from time to time it would result in a goal against. But given that he would score, you know, 200 points per season, it was forgivable. (That sounds ridiculous doesn't it? That someone could actually score 200 points per season? It did really happen.)

And so coaches would insist on getting the puck deep and chasing it. And there's some advantages to this process. If you don't recover the puck, the opponent has 200 feet to go and you have, in theory, at least three men back to defend plus a goalie. And after doing it 50 times, you might turn the puck over and feed it to someone in front of the net and you might score. It's a safe process. And it's a doctrine that Don Cherry, formerly of the Canadian Broadcast Corporation now on Rogers Sportsnet Hockey Night in Canada, continually insists young coaches follow. But it should be pointed out that Cherry's favourite player, Bobby Orr, was not a dump and chase player. He often led the rush from end to end and made his key plays at the blue line. Of course he was so good it didn't matter if he turned it over because he'd get it right back. Cherry's dump and chase philosophy when he was coaching in Colorado didn't save him but he did become a spectacular broadcaster. But that notion of dump and chase has stuck, mainly because it's the safe play, and Cherry preaches it every Saturday night.

And so the objective of the game is to keep your cards as close to the vest as possible and hope you can score first. Once you get up a goal, because the goaltenders are so darned big, it's really hard for the other team to score. Especially if you start to defend the 1-0 lead and not just play it safe but actively trying to defend a 1-0 lead and there is a difference. Before the goal you might be two men in deep and now after the goal you are only sending one man in deep to forecheck. Your chances of gaining the puck are obviously cut in half but your chances of getting caught on an outmanned rush are diminished. Play it safe. And it's one thing to tie the game up and it's quite another to go ahead with the lead. That requires two goals. And so what happens is the team trying to force the issue to tie the game starts pressing, turns the puck over and the defending team, with at least four men back, can pounce the other way.

None of this defensive thinking works if a blast from 50 feet can make it behind a goalie. None of it works.

Because if you think about it for a minute, your whole premise of play is based on the fact that it's really hard to score a goal. If all of a sudden the element of surprise or chance is put into play it destroys the whole defensive structure. And that's what used to happen. Montreal Canadiens star Guy Lafleur would roar down the right side and blast a slap shot from just inside the blue line and it would usually find the back of the net. Or at least there was a real shooter's chance of a goal. Likewise for Jari Kurri of the Edmonton Oilers. He could literally stop that puck on a dime and in an instant fire a no look slapshot top left corner before you could bat an eye. Gretzky made a living rolling down that wing and slapping it. His shot wasn't even that hard. But it was delivered in a blink of an eye and unusually accurate.

After one game Gretzky was asked what he saw of the goalie before he shot the puck. He replied that he didn't see the goalie. Goal scorers only see the availability of the net. The goalie is a blur and the net is in pure focus. You really don't have more time than a butterfly has to flap its wings. It's an instantaneous move and it's unlike anything else in sport. It does not exist anywhere with the possible exception of tennis. Both bodies are moving while directing a tool towards a ball or puck. Except these people do it on ice.

Without question NHL athletes are the best in the world. To a man or woman, every single one of them, I can guarantee, can play football, baseball, basketball, tennis or racquetball or any game you choose to name. And I guarantee it will shock you how good they are even if they've never played that sport beforehand. The required athletics in hockey is superior to any other sport. Period. There's baseball in the game (catching the puck or batting the puck out of the air or deflecting it or shooting it); there's basketball in the game with post ups, picks, zone defenses, blocking out; there's boxing in the game; there's a physical element equal to football. It is the ultimate sport.

All the things these amazing athletes can do have been eliminated by goaltenders with a huge advantage over the shooter who is left with few options. And to be fair, goaltenders became really good at their craft. No other position in any other sport advanced as much as the NHL goalie over the past 30 years.

Now the game is like watching a dog chasing its tail. Once the chance goal was eliminated the game spiraled downwards. It's the chance goal you can't coach against. When Guy Lafleur crossed the blue line and wound up for a slapshot, there wasn't much the opposition coach could do other than cross his fingers. The amount of net available to Lafleur and his high degree of talent meant that even from 50 feet out he had a good chance of blowing it past the goaltender who was reacting because that's what goalies did. A goalie's defense was his lightning fast glove hand and immense courage under fire. They played the percentages on shots, dekes and breakaways. They knew an opposing player's tendencies and played hunches. They didn't cover 95% of the net simply by showing up for work.

Hockey at its highest level was free flowing. It can't really be coached unless you equal the playing field for all teams. And that's what has happened. Every team has exactly the same goalie doing exactly the same thing with every team playing exactly the same way. There's nothing unique from one team to another. Every goalie has around a .918 save percentage. So if you know .918 going into a game then you can coach around it. All of a sudden the chance goal is eliminated and now you can concentrate on defense. Before this period there were offensive minded teams. Remember Roy started his career at an .875 save percentage and he was good.

So teams needed both offense and defense. The Montreal Canadiens with Guy Lafleur of the 1970s and the New York Islanders with Mike Bossy of the early 1980s were perfectly balanced hockey teams. The Edmonton Oilers of the 1980s were offensive machines but could play defense well enough to win in the playoffs. All of that ability to score disappeared with the goaltender advantage. Coaching up until the advent of the giant goalie was like holding a paper bag full of water. It was impossible to hold in your hands. It would leak. Teams could not be water tight through an entire game. And therefore the idea was to score goals and play hockey. In 2017 the Penguins led the NHL with 278 goals. Only one team scored less than 278 goals in 1985.

A lot of people will claim the talent level wasn't as good in 1985 as it is today. There is the argument the 5th and 6th defensemen in those days couldn't skate and therefore Gretzky got a free goal every night. And everyone had a goon, they couldn't play hockey either. I disagree completely with this and suggest to you what has actually happened is that the talent levels of the best players have dissipated so that it looks like the bottom level players have improved in comparison to the old days. In fact, the bottom level players are exactly the same as they were 50 years ago. But that top tier of player has disappeared and so it only appears as though the tide has risen across the board. It has not. I recognize people who played in the league then and follow it now may disagree and I fully expect they would. A lot of them have their own kids in the system and if they came out and said, "these kids today, they suck crap" then who are they criticizing? Themselves and their kids. They're trying to manufacture an NHL player as much as or more than any other parent.

Often times you can't see the forest through the trees and it's usually Canadian ethics to be humble so you'll rarely see former players criticizing modern day players. That's part of the problem. They need to forget the politeness and stand up and voice concern and loudly. The other factor contributing to the lowering of the talent pool are the rule changes which I discuss later.

The defensive argument and defensive teams are certainly not new to the NHL. Roger Neilson attempted to clamp the game down. He was probably the first coach to be defensive only in hockey history and generally it was not successful. But he had brief success in 1982 with the Vancouver Canucks making the Finals by protecting a hot goalie. But it wasn't sustained success. The goalie hadn't advanced far enough until Patrick Roy single handedly delivered a Stanley Cup to the Montreal Canadiens in 1993.

Roy carried the Cup two more times in Colorado. He was by far the best goalie the NHL has ever seen or will ever see in our lifetimes. His teams in Colorado depended on his backstopping as they attacked under a Marc Crawford coached hockey team. They were the last of the full attack hockey teams with a goalie who at times was virtually unbeatable. Roy showed the NHL what could be possible with a goalie almost alone. And yes, Roy had Joe Sakic and Peter Forsberg in Colorado. And they did score goals in bunches. But Forsberg was often hurt. And Roy was the backbone of the team.

Until that time, goalies were part of the team. Billy Smith for the New York Islanders exemplified the ruthless toughness of the team. Tom Borasso personified a Pittsburgh Penguins powerhouse of calmness and professionalism. Ken Dryden of the Montreal Canadiens at times appeared aloof and bored. But Roy changed everything. All of a sudden everyone wanted a Patrick Roy who played this butterfly system and was virtually unbeatable. And after Brodeur everyone wanted a goalie first system. Now you could score one or two goals and make it stick. Beforehand you needed a Lafleur or a Bossy or an Orr to overcome a deficit. Roy proved that at times a goalie was all you needed.

If you drafted a giant goalie and played a defensive system you had a great chance of winning a Stanley Cup. And if you drafted enough of these giant goalies, you could just keep plugging them in, one after another, such as the Penguins in 2016 and 2017 along with the Nashville Predators. It almost didn't matter about the name on the back of the jersey or the front of it. They became interchangeable and that means boring. It went from Roy to nameless in 15 years.

THE TRAP

In 1987, American Lou Lamoriello arrived in New Jersey as general manager. He drafted Martin Brodeur in the first round in 1990 and hired Jacques Lemaire in 1993. The Trap began in earnest in 1994, ironically at the same time the NHL was cresting on the greatest ever hockey series between the Rangers and Canucks. The chapter on hockey's glory years was closing as the "Dead Puck Era" began.

I'm not saying Lamoriello didn't like hockey, but he came at it from a non-hockey background of math, though he did play some high-school hockey and coached college hockey. Lamoriello brought a different perspective to hockey than Saturday night on CBC, coast-to-coast in Canada. He played baseball and hockey in Rhode Island and was an Athletic Director at Providence College and parlayed it into a gig as President of the small market New Jersey Devils in 1987. Gretzky once joked that the organization were clowns because they were a horrendous team.

But Lamoriello would get the last laugh by hiring Montreal defensive guru Jacques Lemaire in 1993 who coached them to a franchise best 106 points and served notice that the defensive first team had arrived and high-flying Oilers type teams were doomed.

Lemaire was a fabulous two-way centre with the
Montreal Canadiens in their heyday from 1967 to 1979.
He was the defensive consciousness of eight Stanley
Cups. In New Jersey with Martin Brodeur in net,
Lemaire ground the game into a pulp with his Trap
system and butterfly goaltender and attention to
defensive detail. Now to be fair to Lemaire, the Trap

wasn't his invention. As former Canucks head coach Pat Quinn used to say, the Trap has been around as long as there has been hockey.

The Trap is when one forward skates deep into the opponent's zone and angles the puck carrier to one side of the rink where the other two defending forwards are waiting for him on that side in the neutral zone so they can't advance up the ice. The opponent is outnumbered and is forced to ice the puck or turn it over. If they turn the puck over either New Jersey would go on a two-on-one man advantage rush or dump it back in and set the Trap again, stifling the game.

Quinn would also say the best way to beat the Trap is to pass it from defenseman to defenseman and go up the other side of the Trap with speed through the neutral zone. However you need nerves of steel and talent to pull it off because if you botch the defenseman to defenseman pass then there's nothing between the opponent who stole the puck and the goaltender. With the expansion of the NHL from 21 teams to 30 teams, the required talent to beat the Trap started to disappear as it was too difficult for teams to ice four defensemen who could pull the feat off. This began the "Dead Puck Era" which I would argue hasn't left despite rule changes by the NHL.

Lemaire and the Devils hit the NHL like a ton of bricks. There were outcries from fans bemoaning their boring play. Even fans in New Jersey often didn't attend games (leading to team financial difficulties.) Lemaire had them playing iron-clad defensive structures to the letter T. They checked Mario Lemieux into the ground. They collapsed offensive teams like a deck of cards. Once they got up a goal it was lights out. They almost took out the highest payroll team in the NHL, the New York Rangers, in 1994. And in 1995 the New Jersey Devils held the President Cup Trophy winning, high payroll, Detroit Red Wings to just 17 shots and won Game 1 of the Finals series and rolled to the Stanley

Cup. Small market teams took notice and joined the defensive parade. Teams which had held fast to offensive styles began losing and eventually capitulated, turning to the Trap for help. And then it began trickling downwards.

Hitherto this point, the feeder system for the NHL, the American Hockey League and before it went defunct the International Hockey League, were leagues almost exclusively devoted to improving skills of a hockey player to get them up to the NHL with their parent club. If they couldn't score 50 goals in the minors they weren't likely to get 30 goals at the NHL. It isn't the case anymore. In 2017 the AHL was led in scoring by Wade Megan of the Chicago Wolves with a stunning 33 goals. Not to pick on Wade but in years gone by that would be considered terrible. It's as hard to score in the minors today as it is to score in the NHL, possibly harder. A 25 goal scorer in the AHL translates to the same in the NHL almost proportionally say third or fourth in league scoring.

So what happened, I think it's safe to conclude, is that "defensive structure" crept into the minor leagues and became the only reason to be in the AHL. A player was in the AHL to get better in their own zone only. Coaches really started caring less about a player's offensive capabilities instead almost exclusively their defensive capability. And then it trickled down to the Canadian junior league levels which is the feeder system of the NHL. There were only five players in the Major Junior Western Hockey League with over 50 goals in 2016/17, and those five just got to 50 goals. In 1984 Ray Ferraro led the league with 108 goals and Cliff Ronning had 69. It's quite a drop from those levels.

Not only did you have coaches at both the minor leagues and junior leagues wanting to become defensive gurus as they saw it was the only way to become a coach in the next level up, players who had played in the NHL under this defensive structure became coaches in the junior and AHL ranks. And of course people copy a winner and it trickled right down from there to the atom and pee wee ranks which should never have happened. Every other sport teaches kids the fundamentals such as how to hit, how to catch, offense and defense. All of a sudden in the amateur ranks you had coaches trying to emulate the Trap with 10-year-olds so they could coach the next level up. The focus is defense. So if you're focusing on defense, and at all levels of hockey, then offensive players are weeded out and discarded systematically.

What you need in a Trap system is a defensively conscious forward with size, strength and speed who won't do anything stupid with the puck, also known as displaying their talent. Under a coach like Pat Quinn, the forwards had the freedom to improvise in the offensive zone but had to listen to him in the defensive zone. That was the norm for some 75 years but as Lemaire moved forward in New Jersey and their system brought success the game began to unravel. Offensive juggernaut teams evaporated under the Trap. Not only were they turning the puck over to a New Jersey Devils Trap team, the Devils were outscoring the rest of the league, albeit at a modest pace. Teams across the league began to crumble under the pressure of the Trap. Beautiful teams like the Oilers began to talk 200 foot games.

In 1998 Lemaire left hockey and the game could have recovered but he returned in 2000 to coach the expansion Minnesota Wild. The beautiful early 2000 Vancouver Canucks with the Pineapple Express line of Todd Bertuzzi, Markus Nasland and Brendan Morrison and the Sedin brothers on the second line coached by the high-flying Marc Crawford were cut down at the knees by the Lemaire coached Minnesota Wild in 2003. The path Mario Lemieux warned the NHL about taking back in 1995 had arrived everywhere. It was heading down a path of bleakness with this Trap under Lemaire but to no avail. Winning was everything. Even though the New

Jersey Devils were not putting people in the seats they were winning and it was undeniable. When the Lemaire coached Wild would go on the road the host fans, such as Vancouver, would groan at the thought of yet another game with the Wild. The Western Conference started to compete with Lemaire with team after team going "all-in" on the defensive structure to compete with the Wild. There was no denying Lemaire was damned good at his job. He was too good and teams wanted a Lemaire. Even the high-flying Canucks fired Crawford and replaced him with Alain Vigneault, a Lemaire partisan, and he served up some of the hardest hockey to watch in NHL history in his first few years.

After the NHL strike of 2004/05 and 2012/13 new rules were implemented to try to open the game up and return hockey to its glory days. No matter what the NHL did, the moves backfired and defensive structure had a vice grip on the league. We know this because they tried in 2005 and again in 2013 to no avail. There was some improvement in the Eastern Conference which seemed to embrace the open game again but not so in the Western Conference where Lemaire had entrenched a defensive structure from top to bottom.

What does more damage to the game is the Trap trickling down to minor hockey. As previously stated, hockey at the very highest level is an art form. Art can't and shouldn't be constricted. And it can't conform. And in many cases it can't be explained. It is the expression or application of human creative skill and imagination to be appreciated for their beauty or emotional power. Pavel Bure lifting the puck into the air from behind the net, throwing it over the net with his stick, and skating around to the front of the net to hit it out of the air and into the net is the definition of art (although he missed the puck.) No one could have seen that coming. He saw a problem of getting to the front of the net from behind the net and a defender on either side confronting him. His imagination took hold and he flipped the puck high in the air, over the goalie, into the crease in front of the net where he had skated while people watched the puck and he swung at it with his backhand. It lifted hundreds of thousands of people out of their seats or couches to shout in unison: "Oh my God, did he just do that?" Or could anyone stop from laughing as Mario Lemieux adeptly stick handled the puck through Boston Bruin's defensemen Ray Bourque's feet on the way to a goal? There was nothing else you could do but laugh at the pure magic of Mario. Or watching Wayne Gretzky stop in a corner and throw a puck, seemingly to no one, only to see, two seconds later, an Oiler winger swoop in and put the puck in an empty net. There was no way it should have been possible but Gretzky saw something no one else did.

Gretzky was art on ice. He knew where the puck was going to be and where everyone else was going to be before they did. But could you imagine today if any hockey player threw the puck up the ice like that? You don't see it anymore. I would argue the reason you don't see it is because these players can't do it. They haven't played the game at a high enough level to turn it into art. It's no wonder they haven't developed to the same place as Lemieux, Bossy or Orr. They're not allowed to develop their art and this is the trickle down of 23 years of preaching defensive hockey at all levels to extremes.

When I was a kid we almost never had defensive coaching, especially for practices. There was no structure or limited structure in the practices. A coach would come out, dump a bucket of pucks on the ice, and go sit on the boards and smoke and yack with a friend. From time to time they would circle out, steal a puck from you, laugh as you tried to get it back, push you away, pat you on the head, laugh some more as they skated away from you. At least half the practice was a free-for-all. After the free-for-all you might have three on two line drills and a scrimmage. There were the occasional words of wisdom which had impact. But they would skate around the rink mostly playing with the kids, trying to help them learn to skate a bit better. It was really fun. I loved every practice. I couldn't wait to get on the ice. I couldn't wait to play with the puck.

And then there were the "open ice" times of the day at the arena where everyone was welcome and you could just scrimmage with all ages. Bring a puck, stick, gloves, skates. I know in bigger urban centres this seems impossible but in small towns it's actually a thing. A few players from my small hometown went on to the NHL I believe because of the availability of this scrub hockey. Several more could have and should have but no one scouted there since it was so far out of the neck of the woods, as it were. I wasn't an NHL goal scorer. But that same system created multiple 50 goal scorers for decades across Canada. Endless hockey games without coaches.

The point I'm trying to make is hockey can't be forced. Learning hockey is a private venture. Well, it can be forced but you don't end up with artists. There's more than one way to skate. There's more than one way to shoot. There's more than one way to hit. The combinations are endless. Well they were endless until the Trap started to trickle down. And greed took its toll as parents started seeing dollar signs in their kids as NHL pay cheques hit the millions.

And now instead of leaving kids to learn at their own pace and learn their own system of the art form they began to be fit into a box. Conform to this. This is what you learn at this time. You must look like this when you skate. You must shoot like this. You must spend more time lifting weights and less time playing hockey. And the reason being is that the Trap began to show the "coaching" as the premiere product of hockey. All of a sudden coaching was more than walking into a dressing room and yelling or telling a joke.

Coaches were desperate I think for a long time to justify their reason for being behind a bench. And now all of a sudden the Trap delivered their case. The Trap said coaches mattered. The Trap said, ah hah! I can also make money in the NHL. I can communicate a form of defensive structure that will allow a team with mediocre talent to win championships. And monkey see, monkey do, it hit the minor leagues and then the junior leagues and unfortunately it hit the kids square in the face.

I remember one time about 10 years ago walking my daughter into a local ice rink which has a couple of ice sheets in the building. I was taking my daughter to rent skates and hit the ice at public skating. At the same time we were heading into the doors a team of, I'm guessing, 12-year-olds, was entering to use the other ice sheet. They were all dressed in suits and ties and the coach was a very serious young man with a grave chin, his game face locked on solidly. I saw them on the ice when my daughter and I left. This was a practice.

They were headed to a practice wearing suits and ties at the age of 12. I stood there for a while watching this very serious coach blowing his whistle, standing on the ice, yelling, screaming with these young kids doing exactly what he says, when he says. He was holding a clipboard taking very serious notes. I left the arena with my daughter glad she wasn't of that gender. I couldn't imagine leaving my son in such a place of torture. Who could enjoy their time on the ice? How do you fall in love with the game under this regiment? You would absolutely learn to conform or learn to leave hockey. There it was, mid 2000s, defensive structure on display, their little suits and ties hanging in the dressing rooms. No ghetto blaster blaring the Ramones, the coach laughing, smoking, joking with his assistant, all of the children without a care in the world, learning their own way of learning the game. Now it was a coach yelling orders and little drones following them. Just like the US Marine Corps.

As I think back on the world I was a part of before it changed I realized how lucky I was to be a part of that history. I really loved hockey. My coaches imparted to me the biggest lesson of life - enjoy yourself, do it your way, and never change. They imparted humour and laughter as the best medicine. They adapted their coaching to kids. There was no attempt to teach Traps or defensive structures or breakout patterns. There was licorice, orange crush, brothers, friends, ice, pucks, frozen breath, cold plexiglass, rusted metal fences, torn skates, wooden sticks used for street hockey, holes in the gloves, helmets that flopped on your face unless you held the strap in your teeth.

My coaches were men and women. They were loggers. They worked for a living. There was nothing pretentious about them. They were the same people you would have found in the country 100 years ago. Work for your pay. And it was risky work. Logging or fishing is the most dangerous profession in the world. And I think it's this immensely difficult work that they do that makes them the best coaches. I'm slipping away from the main point here so I'll bring it back. These are the type of people that if you had told them you have to teach kids to do this, exactly this way, at this time, you would have found yourself without a coach. I know, and hope, there are men and women left in hockey who take the rule book of "coaching" and dump it in the trash can, who roll a cigarette, or take a chew of tobacco, and bark at the kids to go have fun.

Below the age of 14 in hockey, and I think in any sport, there shouldn't be any structure. The primary purpose of the game and practice is scoring goals and to teach the kids friendship and to love their sport in the way that they play it and not to be told they're doing it wrong. I say this because this is how you grow artists. You put down a lot of good soil, dump some seeds in, stamp it with your foot, and step to the porch to see what grows, occasionally watering it.

Now in other sports, having not grown up in a football town, it is possible you need to repetitively teach the fundamentals of the game because in some positions their roles never change. A block for an offensive linesmen is the same today, tomorrow, next week. But it's not true in hockey. There's more than one way to skin a cat, as my dad used to say. So when I walk into a rink today and I see coaches operating from a coaching bible because they have been certified (by God knows whom) I shudder. The Trap led to the justification of the coach which led to the rule book of coaching and certification. Once you certify something and regulate it, then you can kiss off any artist coming up through the system. They won't make it. They can't make it. Of course they can't make it through. They don't conform. You can't pigeonhole them. They see a way to do something and it works and good enough, next problem. Hockey at its core is a set of problems that you have to overcome in order to score a goal. You have to learn to stand on skates, then skate, then move forward, then hold a stick, then shoot a puck, then shoot a puck where there isn't someone standing there with immense goalie pads. There are so many permutations that it can't be restricted without dire consequences.

I'll give you two examples of what I mean. Luc Robitaille of the Los Angeles Kings and Brett Hull of the St. Louis Blues. Robitaille is the highest scoring left winger in NHL history. Or was, I believe he still is at 668 goals. And Brett Hull, with a staggering 741 goals, wouldn't exist in today's game. Robitaille was a terrible skater. Hull was slightly better. So how did they get to the staggering heights they did?

They reached those heights because skating isn't the end all to be all in hockey. Or at least it shouldn't be the bees knees. If you can get there at the right time then good enough and who cares how you look doing it. Robitaille and Hull spent the majority of their time perfecting what they really loved - shooting the puck. And boy did they ever. They had lightning fast wrists.

But they wouldn't get a scout to look at them now because they don't skate the same as the rest of the kids.

Skating is just a tool to get the objective done. It doesn't have to look pretty. But in a Trap system you have to conform. Defensive structure demands the same player over and over again. There's no room for choppy skaters because they need gap control in a Trap system. The game has evolved to the point where everyone must close distances between themselves and the opponent as quick as possible. Skating is their key and not being able to handle the puck is irrelevant because if they did get the puck the objective is to shoot the puck into the corner and chase after it, again using their speed. I fully expect forwards to begin equipping with speed skates (long versions of skates designed for pure straight ahead speed but very difficult to turn quickly with.) The defensive structure of the Trap has led to an obsession with cutting goal scoring opportunities for the opponent. This despite the fact they have monstrous goalies in net who stop the puck easily from anything beyond 20 feet.

Goal scoring opportunities lead to goal scoring opportunities. The corners of the arena are rounded. The glass and boards deflect the puck out one scoring zone and into another sometimes for the other team going the other way. It used to be a play to allow the forward to shoot the puck so the goaltender could catch it and pass it back up to the forwards going the other way. And also by allowing the puck to be shot the opponent is giving up the puck. There wasn't this paranoia about giving up 30 plus shots per game. Under this system if you had better talent you were going to win.

Not until Roger Neilson did a team start to purposefully try to limit shots on net. Until then it was a given part of the game that back and forth hockey would develop. And the team with the superior talent was usually going to win. You never had examples of inferior teams dragging the game into the mud. Bad teams would often try to skate with their superior opponents and try to surprise them. There was honour in the game to give it your best shot and maybe tie the game but at least to give it a sporting chance. There was a real element of entertainment on the ice. It was about entertainment.

Hockey is, or was, the best sport to watch live. Gleaming shirts, loud shouts for the puck, flowing hair either from out of the helmet or without a helmet. It was non-stop movement up and down the ice. The entertainment value was second to none.

Every game was different. Whether it was Guy Lafleur allowed to put on a show on a rainy night in Vancouver or a sunny afternoon in Los Angeles. Fans came to see the stars and they rarely disappointed. Whether it was Mario Lemieux with a cancer hobbled body or Bobby Orr on one knee. It was a show, a marvel, a spectacle.

That entertainment value has been sucked completely out of the current NHL. And yes some of that is because of the helmets they have to wear and the masks that shield us from them, but it's also because every team plays exactly the same way with almost the same amount of talent level. If that weren't the case then how could you explain a John Tortorella getting fired in one year in Vancouver and coaching a terrible Columbus team (that had just fired its coach) the very next year to marvelous success? And his assistant in Vancouver, who also got fired, replaced a fired coach in Pittsburgh and won two Stanley Cups. Two teams fired their coaches, hired two fired coaches, and had success. There's no rhyme or reason to the NHL anymore. Next man up, next goalie up, next coach up. You can have streaks where a team scores the first goal consistently and wins a Cup and then streaks following where the luck isn't there and they're fired. It's completely random because the teams are so close in talent levels.

Part of what the Trap started was a regimen of discipline because of that all important first goal and defensive commitment. Every team used to have an entertainer, an Eddy Shack, a Tiger Williams, a Dave Semenko, a Bob Probert. They took penalties. Marvelous, marvelous penalties. It wasn't uncommon for them to get over 200 penalty minutes in a year and their antics in the penalty box was something to behold. They understood it was entertainment. It was a night at the opera for beer drinking families. It wasn't a side show, it was THE show. But now the emphasis on defense taken to nth degree means you can't have a pure entertainer on the team. Not that Tiger Williams and the others couldn't play, they scored goals, but they caused chaos and at times were defensively challenged. But hockey needs this chaos to create offense.

Now every single coach says the same thing: "We need four lines that can score." That couldn't be further from the truth. What you really need are four completely different lines bringing different things to the table whether it's a speed line or a physical line or a tough line. But now, because the speed Trap is the be all to end all, every single team wants four lines who can check the puck into the dirt. Close the gap. Angle them off, dump it in, chase it.

Even the current stars of Sidney Crosby and Connor McDavid rarely do anything creative. Their whole game is based on speed rushes. That's why you hear the term over and over again, "It's a young man's game." The younger the game has gotten the worse it is to watch. There's virtually no creativity in the game and almost no one who can do anything with the puck. It's been coached to death. The myth that a 2-1 game can be great to watch is just that, a myth. A 2-1 game is awful to watch. Nothing happens. Soccer on ice.

The one advantage hockey had over every other sport was the element of surprise. Basketball, football and baseball all have the same scenario. Hockey could show you something every night that you hadn't seen before. The permutations of the game provide for a variety of options. Football is pretty regimented and confined.

Basketball is limited by the height of your players. And baseball is, well, let's face it, boring as heck. And while the NHL has taken steps to try to get scoring back in the NHL, the NFL and NBA has introduced scoring back into their games. There is a difference between trying and getting it done.

The crime of the Trap is the players who grew within it. The fact it made it all the way down to minor hockey rinks. It should never have made it to anyone below the age of 20. But of course it trickled down because everybody coaching thinks they're the next Scotty Bowman and so it was the dive into the toilet with no ability to recover even with rule changes. Every ounce of creativity, at least that I can see at the NHL, has been driven out of these kids. Most of them have difficulty making and receiving a 20 foot pass. Most of their passes are in the skates or hit someone in the behind. The snap shot doesn't exist anymore. Nobody has to prove their courage in a fight anymore. Just play the system and rush around like chickens with their heads cut off. There's no time for hockey in this hockey.

COACHES

The Trap sent every coach moving towards defensive structure and defensive structure only. Even offense became a system with keeping a third man high so that you didn't give up an odd man rush the other way. You couldn't overload a side with three or four men to retrieve a puck. God forbid you gave up a three-on-one back the other way because a defenseman got caught pinching. The Trap became all encompassing. Great offensive teams were forced to comply because unless you had a spectacular group of defensemen you weren't going to successfully bust through it. As teams struggled for money, as they often do in the NHL, winning became even more imperative than providing entertainment. Although that seems contrary to a positive business model. You would think if you provided a massive amount of entertainment, even in a loss, fans would come back. But you'd have to stick with that formula for more than four years. And in that time you could, with a modicum of talent, for example a Dave Tippett coached team in Arizona, squeeze a playoff berth and a playoff run out of a Trap team. It's easier to coach the Trap to untalented hockey players than it is to teach people to score goals.

By the time these new aged hockey players make it to the NHL the chances of teaching them to score goals is gone. As I said previously, you don't want them to show any hint of creativity anyways because it's dangerous. There's more to why they can't score goals than just simply the Trap and I'll address some of those issues later on. The impenetrable goaltender combined with the Lemaire Trap and expounded upon by other coaches dragged it down to the abyss. I just also want to be clear I don't blame coaches like Lemaire or Ken Hitchcock or Mike Babcock for dragging the game down. Winning is winning and winning is how you get paid and it works.

Almost every coach who gets into coaching does initially for the joy of hockey. Perhaps they are coaching a son or daughter. But somewhere along the way they catch a bug. And it causes competitiveness to creep in. They move up to coaching a rep team. And if they can win, impress someone, shake someone's hand, they might get into Junior tier 2 hockey. And if they can win there, another step up to Junior tier 1. Then from there why not the AHL? If you can win there well why not the NHL? Minor and amateur league coaches have NHL dreams too. How do you get that introduction? That handshake? By winning of course. It seems like no one is hired on the basis of actually teaching kids to play hockey anymore.

The Quebec Major Junior Hockey League still produces the most offense in the junior leagues. But what do you hear all the time? Well, there's not much defense played there. Perfect! Unfortunately the junior coaches from the Ontario Hockey League and Western Hockey League seem to have a leg up on advancing because they play a more "NHL brand of hockey." Or in other words, a defensive brand of hockey. If you take a look at the amount of francophone coaches in the NHL you won't see enough from the QMJHL. It's a shame. There's nothing more awesome than hearing a NHL coach breakout into perfect French. And their brand of hockey is better. This should be embraced at the NHL level. French is something no other North American sport has. Bilingualism should be a requirement to coach at junior and higher levels in Canada. And for that matter if you're selling in the USA - why not throw some Spanish in as a requirement too?

I'm not trying to cast blame on these coaches who were pretty much forced to follow suit below the NHL ranks. Defense works better than offense when chance goals are eliminated. The Trap is in itself a Trap. Everyone is forced to play the same way or be eliminated. It's a closed system. And coaches terms are finite. The days of Toe Blake only coaching one team, the Montreal Canadiens, are gone. They started to become disposable as the league expanded. With the continued lack of a lucrative American television contract, teams depend on ticket sales. Winning is the best draw to any hockey team. Coaches needed to start formulating for the lowest common denominator as the NHL grew and talent became thinner on rosters and if they didn't make the playoffs they knew they were likely to be fired. The easiest way to deliver a win was to try to get the game to overtime and then a tie.

When the NHL changed the regular season games to a five minute over time period in 1983 they unleashed a ticking time bomb. It coincided with the arrival of Patrick Roy. Eight years later Martin Brodeur would enter the league with the New Jersey Devils and shortly after that the arrival of the tremendous Jacques Lemaire. In 2004, with the Trap taken hold, the NHL started to award points for OT losses and now every team's objective became to get to OT. And how do you increase the chances of getting to OT? You bog the game down.

Real coaching arrived in the NHL. The Devils were confounding teams with their defensive strategy and winning Stanley Cups. New Jersey, affectionately known as the Swamp, was perhaps the best place for this formula to work. Lemaire previously had a brief stint in

Montreal where the fans and players chaffed at his severe structure. In New Jersey he found fertile ground and it took hold. At the same time as this structure started to find hold in the NHL, something was beginning in Canada's coaching ranks. The National Coaching Certification Program started in 1974. It is coach education delivered in partnership with the Government of Canada. Don't get me wrong, I'm not suggesting there shouldn't be some structure to coaching, some regulations. But with any program there comes competition and coaching, as a rule, adheres to guidelines. For example, if you want to coach a rep team above Pee Wee you'll need "high-performance certification 1 training." You'll also need someone who has taken the Hockey Canada Safety Program.

Prior to 1974, coaching was done by amateurs. Moms and dads, grandads and grandmas, farmers, loggers, janitors - every walk of life - with zero training and a love of the game. Each one bringing something completely different to the table. After this time, beginning in the late 1980s, they all started to bring the same thing to the table - certification. Certification means everyone goes through the same basic training. Everyone learns the same thing and teaches the same thing according to lessons and a hand book. So previously all the coaches were self-taught. And afterwards they were all taught the same "proper" way of doing things.

Think about the players who missed the certified coach in minor hockey. Nels Stewart, Henri Richard, Gordie Howe, Bobby Orr, Phil Esposito, Bobby Hull, Mike Bossy, Guy Lafleur, Wayne Gretzky, Mark Messier, Mario Lemieux, Steve Yzerman, Brett Hull, Luc Robitaille, Joe Sakic and to some extent Eric Lindros, just to name a few. And then look at the great players who started hockey in the late 1980s and onwards. All of the stars of the game before that change came from Canada almost exclusively. From the 1990s onwards the game was either dominated by a Canadian goaltender or a European star such as Nikolas Lidstrom, Jaromir Jagr, Peter Forsberg, Mats Sundin, Alexander Ovechkin, Evgeni Malkin, Pavel Bure, Teemu Selanne and Americans such as Jeremy Roenick, Brian Leetch, Chris Chelios and Mike Modano then Patrick Kane and Auston Matthews. America's talent pipeline is getting stronger. Canada's is not. Beforehand, Canada provided the talent. Afterwards, if you want skill you look to other countries to provide it.

Now many people might say, well, other countries are playing the game much more than they were before and therefore Canada won't have a stranglehold on the top of the game. Yes that's true for America. They were bound to become the best at hockey due to sheer size and their athletic culture. But that shouldn't have affected what Canada delivers to the NHL only the percentage of the players in the game. And what Canada delivers now is completely void of goal scoring ability.

Sidney Crosby is a hardworking guy obviously taught in all aspects of the game. And he can't score goals. At the height of his career he is at best a 40 goal scorer. That's sad. And Connor McDavid, for all his accolades, has the same difficulty. McDavid is a tremendous skater and does make most passes at full speed, and usually to the right person. He's like a speed rush defensive end in the NFL using blinding speed to get around the tackle. Eventually the tackles figure out the speed rush is all they do and they fade into obscurity. Goals matter. Crosby has never led his team in the playoffs in goals. Neither has McDavid.

And the gaps between Canada's best "franchise" players has widened. Now you're seeing a really good Canadian hockey player being generated every 10 years, possibly. And they're certainly not at the heights of an Orr, Gretzky or Lindros. They've rarely crested 50 goals in Junior hockey where they once easily hit 100 goals. Today's NHL superstars are coming from countries outside of the Canadian coaching manual in their formative years. Three of the top five scorers in the NHL in 2017 came from outside of Canada and it was a great year for Canada.

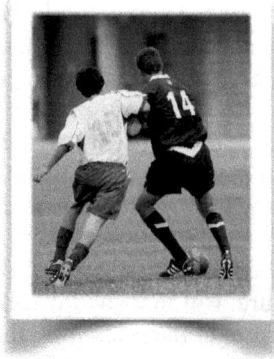

There's another really good example of this occurring in another sport in another country - Dutch soccer. In the 1950s and 1960s kids played in the street before school, during the breaks and after school every single day. Sound familiar? There were no adults or parents. All of the game was played freestyle to win. Winning was everything. As the streets got more crowded and tv started to take priority there were fewer games in the street. As a result, the kids from 1994 onward played a lot less soccer than their dad did as a kid. And of course their men's soccer teams became uncompetitive. They had to make real changes to the way they taught coaching which essentially meant taking the coaching out of it. They changed practices to emphasize scoring goals.

Coaches basically just ask questions and occasionally give instructions or demonstrations. But the practice kept the game going at all times. The philosophy: don't stop to lineup for complex drills kids would hate when there is a finite amount of playing time anyways. In 1986 they introduced 4 v 4 soccer, basically the new face of street soccer. It is a small amount of players on a small field scoring goals! Every lesson or objective had to be taught within the game where they found kids learned quicker instead of drills.

They found the most important thing for the kids was pleasure in playing above technical activities. They found the technical skills were always taught individually and out of context of the game in soccer itself. Everyone finds their own way to accomplish the goal. It may not be what you were expecting but it's how they do it, and that's fine. It doesn't matter what it looks like just get the ball across the line and win! Score goals!

At the age of 18 they started game coaching the efficiency and mental aspects. But only briefly touched on it beforehand. And in the 4 v 4 soccer there is no referee. It's up to the children to control the rules themselves. There is NO GOALKEEPER. After a goal has been scored the player can go right from the back line, goals can be scored from anywhere on the field, penalty kicks take place without a goalie! If they have more than 4 players it's up to the kids to arrange their substitutes. Coaches, parents, adults stay the hell out of it. Let 'em go! Free form soccer.

And from this in 2010 and 2014 they finished second and third in the World Cup in the largest sport in the world. In 1982 and 1986 they didn't even qualify for the World Cup. In 1974 and 1978 they were second in the world. So you can see the proof is in the pudding. The impact tv and other hobbies and over-coaching had on their soccer program almost collapsed it. They just simply didn't have enough kids playing to compete in the 1980s. Those who joined were over-coached as they wanted to cram as much as possible into them while they had a chance.

And I would argue Canada's collapse began in the 1990s and hasn't looked back since. It's been on a steady downward slope. The more the money increased at the

NHL level, the more parents got visions of dollar bills dancing in their heads, and they got more involved and aggressive and coaching handbooks were followed and hockey schools attended religiously and the talent evaporated. And hockey has the added problem of outdoor ice and climate change. Kids are losing the ability to play in a flooded backyard or a frozen pond. And so there's more pressure on ice availability at indoor arenas and that takes money.

Starting with 1990, let's look at the Calder Trophy winners - the best young player entering the NHL.

Ed Balfour, 1990, goalie (Canadian)
Pavel Bure, 1991 (Russian)
Teemu Selanne, 1992 (Finnish)
Martin Brodeur, 1993, goalie (Canadian)
Peter Forsberg, 1994 (Sweden)
Daniel Alfredsson, 1995, (Sweden)
Bryan Berard, 1996, defenseman (USA)
Sergei Samsonov, 1997 (Russian)
Chris Drury, 1998 (USA)
Scott Gomez, 1999 (USA)
Evegni Nabokov, 2000 (Russian)
Dany Heatley, 2001 (German born)
Barret Jackman, defenseman, 2002 (Canadian)
Andrew Raycroft, 2003, goalie (Canadian)
strike, 2004
Alexandre Ovechkin, 2005 (Russian)
Evegni Malkin, 2006 (Russian)
Patrick Kane, 2007 (USA)
Steve Mason, 2008, goalie (Canadian)
Tyler Myers, 2009 (USA)
Jeff Skinner, 2010 (Canadian)
Gabriel Landeskog, 2011 (Sweden)
Johnathon Huberdeau, 2012 (Canada)
Nathan MacKinnon, 2013 (Canada)
Aaron Ekblad, defenseman 2014 (Canada)
Aratemi Panarin, 2015 (Russia)

Now keep in mind the Kontinental Hockey League started in 2008 and NHL general managers became reluctant to draft superior talent in Russia because they didn't need to come to the NHL. And of course the rise of Vladmir Putin and we don't need to go down that road.

So from 1990 to 2015 the forwards were Skinner, Huberdeau and MacKinnon, all after 2008, all after NHL GMs began shying away from Russia. You can argue to add Dany Heatley and I would accept that because Heatley is essentially Canadian. His career fizzled after a promising start in Atlanta. There is essentially no Canadian star drafted and instantly ready for the NHL at a meteoric sustained pace since 1990 such as a Jaromir Jagr or Peter Forsberg or Pavel Bure.

Canada does have Crosby but he has never scored 50 goals in a balanced schedule. Remember, he never played the best teams for 80 percent of his career. He played the Vancouver Canucks three times in his first eight years. Same with Chicago Blackhawks. And that's unfortunate for Crosby because no one can look at his statistics and say they're legitimate. Is he a good player? As I've already said, he's the hardest working plumber in the history of the game. He also epitomizes what's wrong with the game today as a manufactured player. Some of you may be saying, what about Connor McDavid? In his first year he broke his collar bone. In his second year he was passed on his own team by German born Leon Draisaitl. And he was 25th in the NHL in goal scoring. The jury is definitely out on McDavid, I'm sorry.

But I am referring to Calder Trophy winners to prove a point. There is nothing coming and has been nothing in the Canadian pipeline for years. And when you see the collapse of the Czechoslovakia hockey pipeline because their country split and for economic reasons there hasn't been any great Czech since Marian Hossa of the Chicago Blackhawks that's a problem. It's a huge problem. So you have a NHL that has lost Russia and Czechoslovakia as feeder leagues and the Trap eliminated Canada as a feeder system of high-end talent.

The Canadian pipeline of superstars dried up and you can see it, or lack of it, coming out of Canadian junior leagues. Guy Lafleur scored 130 goals in his draft year and played for the Montreal Canadiens next year. Mario Lemieux scored 133 goals in his last year of junior and played for the Pittsburgh Penguins the next year. Sidney Crosby was down to 66 goals in his final year of junior. Connor McDavid fell even further to 44 goals. While Crosby technically crested 50 goals once, it's highly unlikely McDavid will approach 50.

So by looking at Calder Trophy we can clearly see Canada continued to produce goalies and really good complimentary players but no superstars. Part of that is the Trap driving the offense out. Part of it is a smaller pool of players playing hockey, who are playing less hockey because of competing interests which didn't exist three decades ago. And those that are left playing hockey are being coached. And I don't want to demean those wonderful volunteers who dedicate themselves to the game and the kids. What I do want to demean is the thought process that hockey can be coached. I think the results are pretty clear it can't be coached other than loose sets of instructions. This is a game for artists. This is not a game for plumbers. The ice is a canvas. The game is an imagination.

200 FOOT PLAYERS

There's absolutely no reason in hockey to have 200 foot players. The opposition has three forwards coming down the ice. You have two defenseman and one goalie. So it's still three on three. Even if a player is left completely open the goalie in today's game stops the puck 92 percent of the time. And that forward is playing in a finite environment. It's finite. Where's he going to go? Those forwards are coming back. He has at best two seconds before someone is on him.

Where on Earth did the urgency come from to create these 200 foot players? If the goal is to score goals, and the net is on one side of the ice, wouldn't it be more logical to create 10 foot players? Anyone can hustle back into their own zone including offensive players and there are defenseman on the ice earning a living. And if you turn the puck over, don't you want the person getting the puck to be as offensively talented as possible? Maybe this silliness of defensive specialists started with wanting a whole team of Montreal Canadiens' Bob Gaineys that Lemaire appreciated as a hockey player. But there's no Bob Gainey without Guy Lafleur.

Basketball crept into hockey in the form of zone defenses but in the NBA they don't have a goalie guarding the net. Hockey does. NHL teams now play a form of zone which was banned in the NBA. And as goalies got better, as the Trap evolved into the Five Man Collapse system coaches needed more and more defense to counter the other team's more and more defense. The Five Man Collapse system (an NBA zone defense) is putting five of your players laying on the ice in front of your goalie in either the 2-3 or 3-2 format.

It got to the point where you had coach Ken Hitchcock in Dallas trying to get Brett Hull to concentrate on defense where Hull had spent his whole life working on offense. Steve Yzerman became a "better 200 foot" player under Scotty Bowman, sacrificing offense to help defensively. Of course there's nothing to say in either of these examples that if Bowman or Hitchcock had helped Hull or Yzerman to score even more goals that it wouldn't have been successful too. But nobody ever says that. Then when Hull and Yzerman won Cups you saw teams using it as an example of it working. Currently the Washington Capitals coach Barry Trotz is trying to get "Alex Ovechkin to play a 200 foot game." Anybody looking from outside the hockey world would simply say, "Why not just help Ovechkin to score more?" But that thinking is gone in hockey.

Goal sucking is one of the best plays in hockey and it got thrown out the window by the zone defense requiring 200 foot players. (Goal sucking is when the offensive player sneaks out of his zone early getting behind the opposing defenseman at the centre ice line and hanging out at the red line to catch a pass and go in for a breakaway.) The NHL tried to get it back with the removal of the redline but it didn't work. It can't work because the players are all back in their zone defense blocking their own net.

Another reason it hasn't worked is the lack of offensive players in the NHL capable of getting behind a defenseman and receiving a bullet pass on the fly and the lack of offensive defenseman capable of passing it to him. Even if there were stars in the game they wouldn't be allowed to leave the zone early to try the play. It's kind of like baseball coaches never green lighting a player to swing on a 3-0 pitch. And since the defensive game is stressed so much players are so worried about leaving the zone early that very few of them dare to leave the defensive zone before the puck. In football terms it would be like never trying a 40 yard pass to spread the defense out.

The objective now is to put all five players, preferably laying on the ice it seems, in front of their own goaltender within 20 feet so it's impossible for the opposition to get a clear shot on net. They exert all of their energy to stopping the puck. When they get the puck, they only have energy to skate to centre ice and dump the puck in and change up. They're so far back in their own zones they pose no threat from an offensive point of view. Moving the blue line into the neutral zone compounded the problem. The kill zone, as I call it, is much smaller. The blue line used to be closer when you were playing defense. So they've put the offense "jump off area" further away.

Before the Trap the neutral zone was an offensive area. It was fair game for the players. Offensive players learned to gather speed and make their moves in this kill zone. And of course the NHL made it smaller by moving the blue lines towards the centre of the ice. The Trap requires strict play in the neutral zone and there's no room for creativity. Player's practice times are limited. If you take that time and divide it into three sections, defense, neutral zone and offense, now you're cutting an offensive player's learning time in two-thirds. Now defense in the neutral zone is a thing. And when you're teaching defense you're doing it at the expense of offense.

Gap control became the "in" thing in all three zones (closing the distance between a player without the puck and the one carrying it.) Rush at him at full speed and the faster the player is so he can close the gap, then all the better. The objective is to get the puck carrier to dump the puck in so that you can retrieve it, and they can force you to dump it in. And that's how the NHL evolved into Red Rover.

So when you're in this maddening game of Red Rover speed is the necessity, not skill, and definitely 200 foot players. One-on-one moves are almost completely gone. Players don't want to turn the puck over. The objective of the game was to beat someone and get to the net. Not anymore. The objective now is to not make a defensive blunder or you'll be sitting on the bench a long time. Coaches have never been impressed with defensive mistakes. However, coaches like a Pat Quinn would put the player back on the ice right away after a mistake so the player had an opportunity to save face and make a better play. He was an offensive coach. Offensive coaches or what can be called a player's coach are now few and far between in the NHL. Just the fact "players' coaches" are almost eliminated from the NHL should bother hockey fans. Well, whose coach are they now if not for the players? That's very disconcerting.

Every team plays a variation of the Trap today. And it is a Trap. It's waiting for the player who is assertive instead of reactive. If you try to make a play and you fail the consequences are a long ride on the bench. And for players on the bubble in the NHL, the so-called third or fourth liners, it could mean a trip down to the AHL. And so a quarter of an entire team goes on the ice and doesn't think of themselves as entertainers in the NHL, rather as someone who has to preserve a job. The NHL is nothing more than a race for defensive supremacy in a non-traditional way. And that way is to skate the puck deep into a safe area.

Every game in the regular season today is what would have been seen in the playoffs 25 years ago, minus the goals. And then the playoffs are taken to further extremes today. The regular season used to be a form of entertainment. Players took the term entertainment to mean providing entertainment to the fans in terms of offensive, exciting hockey. And I'm sure most players and teams still think of providing entertainment to the fans today. But if the opponent won't play ball with you and you try to open it up and you lose a ton of games then there won't be any fans in the stands. The pressure keeps mounting and the game gets further from entertainment.

As the league got watered down through expansion, as the Trap took hold, as larger goalies made it more difficult to score, offensive coaches lost their jobs. And the downward loop continued to the point where every action in the defensive, neutral and offensive zones is scrutinized on an iPad while the player's still sitting on the bench. Now you need the proverbial 200 foot player. You need five defensemen on the ice, two isn't good enough. Every player has to block shots. Every player has to close gaps. Every player has to be defensive in the offensive zone. No risk hockey. Shut it down, play for the 0-0 draw if you can. Get it to the extra point. Check, check, check and check some more. Give it 110% for 25 seconds and get to the bench. The 200 foot player.

Offensive players need to coast. They act like a hawk on the ice. The entire rink is only 200 feet long so they're never far away. Constantly circling just out of the play they analyze and wait for their moment to strike. They are kids usually with an older brother who have learned to give the bigger kids their room and to pounce on the puck when given half a second of opportunity. They preserve their energy for that perfect moment when the puck arrives and the defenders have been on the ice for 30 seconds going flat out while they have been coasting around waiting. Nowadays they would be labelled floaters and wouldn't make it onto a midget rep team. It certainly would not be allowed at the NHL.

Russian Alex Ovechkin in Washington is a good example of a hawk. But they have pressured him to become a 200 foot player. In 2016/17 season he fell to

33 goals and 69 points from 50 goals the previous year. His goal production has decreased but the Capitals team success in the regular season went up. They won the President's Trophy. And they failed to get out of the second round of the playoffs because they couldn't score goals. The one helpful thing he could do for his team was eliminated in an effort to get better in the defensive zone and for what purpose I have absolutely no idea. It would seem to me that scoring your way out of a goal deficit would be the way to overcome a deficit. Being an overwhelmingly good offensive player is its own defensive deterrent.

In the past, teams had to cover these immense weapons with a player shadowing him which would open up even more ice for the offensive hockey player. But the Trap forced the rest of the team to become vulnerable and even the mighty Lemieux fell to the Trap in New Jersey as he could not overcome the hacking, whacking and mugging that went uncalled and undeterred. And I know, every year there is a crackdown. But come the playoffs things change.

And so the light went on around the league. No longer did you have to wait for a franchise centre to arrive via the draft. You could just check and Trap them into the dirt by abandoning any thought of playing hockey yourselves. You would have thought it would be called unsportsmanlike hockey and thus the Trap team would have been penalized repeatedly for this tactic but the theory is you can't call everything and the league never asked the referees to call it unsportsmanlike conduct. With three 200 foot forwards and two defensive defensemen you can put a barrier around the oversized and stuffed goaltender which makes it virtually impossible to play hockey. First mistake loses the game so don't do anything risky, don't do anything stupid, avoid the kill zone, slap it in, chase it, get back in front of your goalie.

It's an absolutely mindless way to play hockey. There's no imagination required. It's the same thing over and over again waiting for the fluke goal or the goal mouth scramble that resembles a rugby scrum more than a hockey play. It's a wonder they need the ice cleaned between periods nowadays with the way players flop on the ice blocking passes, not shots, but passes, and if you end up cut blocking the offensive player trying to make a play, oh well. There's no penalty ever called for cut blocking on what is plainly an unsportsmanlike play. You see this all the time with the sliding defensive player taking out the oncoming forward's feet. You might as well take the unsportsmanlike conduct rule out of the book and burn it and take the Lady Byng (for most sportsmanlike conduct during the regular season) and throw it away. The result of this sliding around is that no one wants to move the puck into the slot where a forward can throw himself on the ice and block the pass possibly causing a turnover and an outmanned rush the other way, which is rarely an outmanned rush anyways.

As the numbers of offensively gifted players decreased so did the ability to give and go with an equally talented hockey player especially with expansion affecting the dispersion of a limited pool of players. The days of Adam Oates feeding Brett Hull with a precision pass in a perfectly quiet place on the ice are long gone. Teams can barely ice two offensive minded hockey players at the same time and it's not enough to feed the engine. In order to play an offensive game you need a hawk, a pure passer and a third forward who can think with them and be where he can cover the hawk and that means at times taking real chances in the offensive zone to get open for that offensive generator who operates very much like a quarterback on an NFL field. He has to see the whole field and get time to make his move or pass. The field has to be opened up. But how can you open up that field for him when you're just continuing to run the ball up the middle? Every player has another player within a supporting ice area. It's a backup. There is someone to make sure the other team can't exploit a case of the other 200 foot player making a mistake.

So what you're doing with this theory is making the ice incredibly small. Your goal is not to spread the offense and open ice for the hawk but to collapse to each other so no one has to make more than a 20 foot pass. Of course there's not going to be separation which is what an offensive hockey player needs to score goals. You could pretty much throw a blanket over the players on the ice today and capture all ten of them. And since you're moving within this blanket you're always time limited. You'll often hear coaches talking about this gap control. It can be beaten by offensive hockey players playing with other offensive hockey players who can exploit knowing what the opposition is going to do. But you need someone else who can move with you. Henrik and Daniel Sedin, Swedish, are probably the best two hockey players of the past 20 years, and they have given tremendous demonstrations on how this system is easily exploited and destroyed. But you need two of these hawks and a highly skilled winger with them who can bury the puck when they create the open ice. And as we've seen with the elimination of the kill zones by eliminating the red line, the Sedins have been slowly diminished in their ability to exploit these less skilled hockey players.

RED LINE ELIMINATION

Now without the redline causing offside passes it really has become the domain of the 200 foot player with speed. And it's exactly what you didn't want if you wanted skill to rein supreme. The one thing highly skilled players can do with the puck is exploit these kill zones, the areas where people had to stop because of an offside. That moment of hesitation or freezing of the opponent is all they needed to make their play and move forward. Now you can rush at these hawks without their ability to use the kill zone because it's on the other end of the rink and even for them it's a difficult pass. What used to be a 20 foot pass tape to tape is a 50 foot hope and a prayer. It's basically telling Troy Aikman of the Dallas Cowboys that his bread and butter 10 foot quick out is gone and every pass must be a 40 yard deep fly pattern. It's not going to work very often because the opponent knows it's going to come.

So what happens is the defender simply moves to his own blue line, keeping everything in front of him, and never gets caught at the neutral zone with a pass behind him. The red line is no longer there. He doesn't have to move up and support his offensive players. He quickly concedes the red line (because it isn't there) and retreats to the blue line. From there he makes sure no one gets behind him. Where are these hawks supposed to make a living? The ice has been tilted so far towards the defender it's almost impossible for the offensive player to do anything.

What is the trademark of a highly skilled hockey player? The ability to give and receive a pass that is perfect. The area where they could work and use this gift was eliminated when the NHL removed the centre ice red line. The two blue lines and the centre ice red line gave three distinct opportunities for the talent to get to work. These are the zones where they can make a defender vulnerable by either making him come forward or catching them standing or causing them to back up. It's where the action happens.

Perhaps these offensive players weren't as fast in a straight line but what they perfected was the ability to start quickly or shift quickly and most importantly to think quickly. Gretzky is a perfect example of this type of player. If the defender backed up too far beyond his own blue line then Gretzky could come in, stop and setup shop at the blue line. If they attacked him he would simply slow down and at the last second pass it to an open winger. Removing the red line means the fastest player, not the best player, has the advantage. This, combined with moving the blue lines forward removed further advantage because now they're further from the net meaning more speed is required.

And there's another red line the NHL tinkered with - the goal line. It used to be called Wayne Gretzky's office behind the net. What did the NHL do? They moved the net forward with the goal line thinking, ah hah! If we make more room behind the net we'll get more people setting up office back there like Gretzky and we'll get more goals. And that's exactly what didn't happen. Now you've made it easier for the 200 foot player to get behind the net and get at the puck mover. There's less room in front and they won't trip on the net trying to get behind it. And yes I understand they tried to make up for this by moving the blue line back into the neutral zone but because the defensive system to combat that is to drop five guys on the ice in front of their oversized overstuffed goaltender, there isn't any more room for someone in Gretzky's office. And also if you make a pass back to the blue line up the middle and, God forbid, miss, you've done the Cardinal sin of creating a turnover because now the defensmen are further away because you backed the blue line up. The only play behind the net now is to bounce it off the boards back to the defensemen who immediately has a speed rusher coming at him and he simply dumps it along the boards back to the corner. The game of Red Rover. The ability of these players to make a one-on-one move has decreased to the point that very few defensemen can confidently shuffle past the speed rusher and get into the slot and score a goal. And to be fair, the defenders are faster by half a second forcing them to move quicker than before. And they've limited the goalie's ability to play the puck (and make mistakes) by putting more lines behind the net.

Compounding the problem of the elimination of these places to hide on the ice, the speed requirement is eliminating all other roles in hockey. You don't have specialty defensemen with offensive ability such as Al MacInnis, Jeff Brown, Brad Park or Larry Murphy. You don't have enforcers to protect the hawks from getting mugged. You don't have the tough defenseman who can protect his players and deliver punishing hits. These players usually had requirements other than pure speed. Those little details eliminated vulnerabilities hawks would look for on the ice. Those vulnerabilities were what they exploited. Once they were eliminated you didn't need the hawk. You just need five speed rushers closing the gap. If they can hold a stick and skate - perfect. A 200 foot player is all you need to stop hockey from breaking out.

It's easier to coach defense than it is offense. Offense is unpredictable. The hardest part about coaching offense is not coaching. It's letting the kids figure out their own way at their own pace and staying out of the way. Defense is a logical equation. If this happens then do this. If you see this happen then go here. Stand here. Watch this lane. Wave your stick. Slide on the ice and block the pass or block the shot. Skate 20 feet in the middle of the ice behind the left winger (left wing lock) and force the opposition to the boards. Stay in front of the defenseman. When you get the puck immediately shoot it in and change.

I'm of the belief that hockey really can't be coached nor should it be coached for best result. But the problem is defensive coaching works in hockey to produce wins although it's a horrific product to watch. So what we do is shut it down before it can begin. Offensive hockey is a creation of chaos. Only when it's played on the edge of chaos can you get amazing results. But if you're determined to shut a game down you sure can.

And to be fair to coaches in a salary cap era you need to use these underage players at 18 to 22 because it's when they are the cheapest on entry level salaries and so you have to dumb the game down to get them involved. Without exception they're clearly not ready to play at the highest levels. Even Auston Matthews who won the Calder Trophy in 2017 had massive flaws such as his inability to pass the puck at even strength. And so you need a style of game into which you can plug and play these "development camp" hockey players.

They almost all go to the same style of "offensive" hockey development camps and learn exactly the same thing and as I previously stated hockey isn't like football. You can't teach "offense" in a package. You have to get on the ice or play ball hockey and fool around without coaches and there's no other way to learn it. Everybody learns their own thing and specializes in their own field. You can't coach it. But you certainly can take these drones and plug and play them into a 200 foot player game. It's a really simple boring game to play.

ANALYTICS

There's people out there who for some reason have gone down a baseball road of trying to determine statistics for every single play on the ice and it's leading to the elimination of the variety of players required in the game. Analytics favours speed skaters. And it has moved into the GM circles at the NHL. Analytics doesn't work for a variety of reasons. But this analytics has led to the determination that 200 foot players produce better results for a hockey team. That's completely not how hockey works. An example would be the thought that blue liners should be small, mobile, and fast puck movers. The Florida Panthers are a perfect example of someone trying this only to fall flat on the ice. Hockey is a vicious game at its heart. Sacrificing size and strength for speed only ends with injuries.

Analytic nerds first and primary claim is that goals don't accurately measure performance. Do I have to go on after that? Where do you think any conversation or analysis that starts by dismissing goals ends? The 200 foot player. I read this article in the USA Today from two years ago explaining analytics that says if a player got two goals in a game you'd think he'd had a great game but what if he just got two lucky bounces and that's all he did in the game? So the premise of analytics is goals don't matter.

The people who generate offense (but don't score goals) are more important than those who actually score goals. I'll put this in basketball terms. Great Canadian basketball player Steve Nash drove offense. But he never won the NBA title because they needed someone to put the ball in the net. In 2016 the Golden State Warriors couldn't get past Lebron James. So in 2017 they signed Kevin Durant who put the ball in the basket and they then beat Cleveland. Golden State had a person who drove offense, their guard Stephen Curry, but no one to put the ball in the net. What analytics in hockey is saying is the guard is more important than the person who puts the ball in the net. In hockey the act of putting the puck in the net is the ultimate act. That's an art form. Goals and only goals matter. There is no offense without the person who can score the goal.

It's my experience there is never a lucky goal. From afar it may look like goal scorers floated all game. But I can tell you from experience that's not how it works. It's almost like they are savants or autistic. It's uncanny how they end up following the game for 50 minutes then out of nowhere they pop two goals in while you're just standing there watching, sweating away, wondering how they're not even breathing hard. It's easy for them. But getting to that level, Masters level, takes years and years of practice. They let the game buzz around them, like a predator watching the herd of antelope, and out of nowhere they strike. They often appear aloof. They often appear disinterested. Often their goals appear lucky. Caught the goalie napping or it bounced off someone's shinpad or butt. They look like they're not trying. They make quick analysis of back checking and determine it's better to conserve the energy and hang back in case of a turnover and quick outlet pass the other way. They quickly determined it's a better play than skating fast for no reason. They may sense the opponent with the puck can't score. It drives coaches nuts because they see the one time they were wrong not the 20 times they were right.

They may have games when the opposition outshoots them all night long. And you have to understand they've factored that in. Believe it or not they're able to analyze the opposition by the way they skate, play, every single little detail goes into their computer. And at the end of the game they have two goals and you look at the "possession" analytic numbers and they're terrible. He "didn't generate offense." Yes, that actually is said in analytics of a goal scorer.

Seemingly there is almost no value today in pure snipers and it has a lot to do with analytics. Teams want 200 foot players who can give you eight goals and 14 assists and can close the gap and "drive" offense meaning when they are on the ice their team gets more shots on net than the other team. So they're measuring the ability of someone to skate fast, get the puck, and shoot from everywhere, regardless if the shot has a chance.

I'd rather have the 70 goal scorer who is outshot every night and I think from an entertainment point of view, we'd all like the 70 goal scorer. Jaromir Jagr was a terrific example of a classic floater. Defensively he had critics. However he also had goals, lots of them, over 700. But he became a 200 foot player and for some strange reason was widely applauded for scoring less. And this is totally true. In his heyday he was considered aloof. Now that he works at all facets of the game, scoring 20 goals per season, well now he's a terrific interview and great for the game. Could it get anymore bizarre than that? The only thing players should be measured for is goals and then first assists and finally second assists. Scoring goals is the key to winning games. Goals matter or they should matter.

Analytic nerds use shots to determine their statistics. If you know anything about hockey then you know there isn't a less reliable statistic than the shot stat. It varies from building to building. Well, I shouldn't say it's the worst statistic because hits might be a worse statistic. What is a hit? What isn't a hit? The point is none of this is measurable to any certainty. In any scientific study garbage in is garbage out. What they're basing their analytics on is not accurate so therefore you can't have any accurate information even if you could measure anything accurately in what is a very artistic sport. Baseball is measurable. It's very static. The hitter stands in the same place every single time. So does the pitcher. Not true in hockey. Analytics also ranks these shots on distance from the net in terms of scoring chances as if they were on the ice and saw what the player saw. A chance from 10 feet can simply be a player throwing the puck at the net knowing there is zero chance of scoring but hoping for a rebound. The same play can be done from 45 feet out. It makes no difference.

The basis for analytics is that incorrect data is gained from goals. It's a low occurrence high-profile event. Well the statement is ridiculous on many levels. If you've ever played hockey you know you can work all night getting open for that one opportunity to put the puck in the net. And it's not based on shots on goal. Goal scorers can constantly go through games not taking shots on net until they do and then it goes in. Now what you have because of analytics are shots from everywhere with no chance of success but it looks like you're super busy and driving offense. It's something the agent can take into negotiations and say, well, he may only score 15 goals but he drives offense because he works really hard getting shots on net. When he's on the ice he's outshooting the opposition. His team is in the offensive zone. He's driving offense! And he's a 10 goal scorer.

It's ridiculous beyond belief. You're rewarding the 200 foot player for getting pucks towards the net. And it's so wrong. An example of why this is wrong is Spartak or the CCCP Russian national team. They would work the puck back and forth in the neutral zone and back to their own zone until the situation was correct then move in to the offensive zone and work the puck for the right shot and their goal per shot percentage was extremely high. That style of play would bring back a terrible analytics score although they won numerous gold medals and international tournaments and national titles. As my dad said, there's numerous ways to skin a cat. This type of hockey is extremely successful and produced some of the best hockey players ever such as Igor Larionov, Sergei Federov and Valeri Kharlamov but they would score terribly in analytics.

Another falsity of analytics is that it produces better information over a long term. That's completely incorrect. I've seen really good hockey players vary their shot totals based on team needs. And it depends on who they're playing, how their own team is doing, and what kind of injuries they're dealing with. A hawk, for example, can change their stripes and become a shot taker game in and game out. And so therefore you would conclude he's disinterested at times, it's a term I often hear. He works hard occasionally. It's completely inaccurate. What you're seeing is someone who's capable of playing various roles on a team, which is highly desirable. I played with a guy who once spent an entire game feeding me the puck in front of the net so I could score a goal. He put about 30 passes on my tape before I scored. You could conclude he was driving offense or a lazy player depending on how you read that. All I can tell you is that he was laughing pretty hard in the dressing room between periods and after the game. They operate at a different level, they play the game differently, and unless you're in that room with the player you have no clue looking from above what was going on. And of course players can purposefully fail on a play to setup something later on in the game. How would analytics know?

Plus minus statistics are extremely accurate and analytics will tell you they are useless. It's complete garbage from people who don't value goals. It varies wildly from play to play. It means it's pretty much impossible to make a judgement on it. Plus minus stat tells you exactly where someone stands. If he's a large minus it's because he can't score goals and is always scored on. It's as simple as that. Analytics nerds will try to find ways to minimize it and blame it on someone else because the plus minus stat tears holes in their nerdiness. It would be better if they actually just picked up a hockey stick and went down to the local arena at noon and played scrub hockey to figure out why analytics is stupid.

The analytics community also doesn't value face-off wins saying it's not worth having a face-off specialist and so Bob Gainey and Ryan Walters and Manny Mulholtra were a waste of time. Again this is completely untrue. Not all face-offs are equal. Sometimes you desperately need to win a face-off and you need a specialist on the team. The other thing it does is demoralize an opposition. Manny Mulholtra on the 2011 Vancouver Canucks was the best in the business and of course when he got an eye-injury 10 games before the playoffs the Canucks basically had already lost the Stanley Cup because they lost Mulholtra. He was spectacular in the face off circle and gave the Canucks such a clear advantage every night it lead to being the best team in hockey in over 25 years.

When these elite face-off men win their face-off it's usually not open for the other team to get right back either, an assumption the analytic community makes. So again you have to play the game to understand the value these players make. Yes, some people just win a face-off then their team loses it right back. It depends on how good their team is and how good the defensmen they play with. If a Jonathon Teows wins a face-off to Duncan Keith in Chicago it's a pretty good bet they keep possession. So you can take the analytics and throw it out the window. Analytics will also say you should value offensive hockey players who possess the puck more than a really good defensive player. And that's pretty much what I'm saying in this book but I didn't use analytics to determine this. I used the observation of what has happened to the game to determine this outcome.

Defensive defensemen will score badly in analytics because they're usually paired with a high-risk offensive defenseman. They turn the puck over. So it will show in the stats that his team gives up more shots when he's on the ice. Well no kidding. That's why he's on the ice.

Another reason analytics fails is who players are matched up against and for how long. In baseball everyone has a set position and a set IF THEN DO logic equation. It can actually be measured. In hockey it is a strategy to purposefully fail. One of the reasons you may do this is to set a player up for an offensive play later on in the game. Or you may play with a hawk and your job is to create turnovers by purposefully playing badly thus forcing the opposition to continue to move along his side until the opportunity arrives. Someone watching above may think, using analytics, that he's doing terrible with his "possession" numbers and ignore the goal in the third period where the turnover they setup throughout the game happened.

However it may be simpler than that reason. You might just be playing against a stronger more experienced player. And a coach may purposefully encourage these match ups for a variety of reasons. He may wish to see if the kids can sink or swim. Or he may be accentuating a learning curve knowing or hoping there will be a payoff at the end of the curve. It would also be known as baptism by fire. The player will get beat often but the coach may see little increments of improvement over a year that encourages him to continue doing it. Sometimes the only way to learn something is to get beaten repeatedly.

And there's the inherent chaos in hockey which makes analytics impossible. There is a coaching system where you encourage breakdown of structure with the hope of causing enough mistakes that you can score. It's especially used in the last few minutes of a game by the team that is down a goal. But what I'm referring to is hockey's buzz factor. You wouldn't see a first baseman in baseball charge to the third base and have the third baseman run to centerfield and have the catcher run to first base and then have the pitcher throw the ball to the umpire. But essentially it's what you often get in hockey. It's a buzzsaw out there. Forwards back, defensemen up, left defenseman on the right forward, goalie in the corner, two forwards laying in the crease playing goalie. Yes fifty percent of the play is static and everyone is in position playing as expected. But then there's the other half of the game where it breaks down. There's so many variables on the ice it forces people out of position. In fact the whole concept of scoring a goal is to pull people out of position to get someone open.

And then there's the biggest reasons hockey analytics fail because the rules change so often how can you possibly analyze anything over time? It requires data which exists in baseball because the rules have not changed in decades but hockey is always changing the rules and playing surface and so it's always a game that is, at most, three years old. So from a scientific point of view there's no value on any science based on three years of data. There's not enough science in the science. Any science you have is worthless because there isn't 100 years of data to go with it as you have in baseball.

Then there's travel. In the Eastern Conference there's virtually no travel. They sleep in their own bed virtually every night. Travel to the West Coast is an exciting adventure. They don't experience fatigue. They can practice more and when they practice it's meaningful.

And the players are fresher for games. Compare that to the Western Conference players especially those in Vancouver or Dallas who face extreme travel. The fatigue is real. Even the announcers for those teams often comment on how the constant time zone travel tires them out and they often say they have no idea how the players make it happen on the ice. If you look at a Vancouver Canucks schedule and compare it to a Toronto Maple Leafs schedule it's quickly apparent they are not similar. And so how do you use analytics to compare players experiencing different fatigue factors?

And then there's the different levels and styles of play in either of the conferences which interferes with any data. For example, at the height of their careers the Sedins of the Vancouver Canucks averaged two points EACH per game versus Eastern Conference teams. For a five year period in their primes they would have been averaging 160 points each per year playing exclusively in the Eastern Conference such as Sidney Crosby played, who averaged 80. I think it's a fair conclusion that because the Sedins played in Vancouver in a very tough Western Conference they are about 600 points behind where they would be if they had played in Crosby's division. You could easily say the same for Joe Thornton of the San Jose Sharks. Thornton might be one of the top 25 hockey players of all time but because he played most of his career in the Western Conference he's not going to end up in the discussion as he rightly deserves. And for older people who remember Marcel Dionne you can probably add 250 points lost due to playing in his timezone in a division with the Oilers.

Analytics is also affected by the divisional play, conference play and inter-conference play in a season. The schedule has changed so constantly you can't get a read on players or data. It matters, it absolutely matters. The Sedins, again for example, played in the toughest conference in hockey so it impacts their data. And if you play in a division where the other four teams are terrible? You're going to see a massive bump in scores. If you play in a division where all five or six teams are heavy dump and chase defend teams then the points and the underlying data are going to be badly skewed.

Crosby had a free pass for most of his career in Pittsburgh where teams tried to play hockey for at least seven years coming out of the strike/lockout of 2004/05 where they implemented new rules trying to boost points such as red line removal and calling everything as it appeared in the rule book (imagine the nerve.) But that's also a sliding curve. The further it got from the strike the game began to change as the referees began to not call as many penalties, in my opinion due to complaints that they were ruining the game by calling the penalties in the book. "Let them go!" was the old adage. So how do you analyze data when nothing is constant from year-to-year? It's not even constant from October to March in any season, ever. The Eastern Conference didn't have Lemaire, Ken Hitchcock, Mike Babcock, Dave Tippett, Darryl Sutter, Joel Quenneville or Alain Vignault who were defensive defensive specialists and who ground games through the ice into the concrete below. So any data you get is going to be influenced not only by where someone is playing but who they're playing and who they're playing for.

Eventually, as witnessed by the Pittsburgh V Nashville Finals in 2017, no matter how hard the NHL tries to open the game up the rodeo comes back. At times it looks like WWF on ice with players flying through straight arms. I like the WWF and the reason I like them is they came out and said, yes, this is acting to a degree. If 300 pound people actually hit each other like they pretend to do the matches would be over in 10 seconds and there'd be a stream of full stretchers out of the arena. Hockey has a rule book but when and where it's enforced isn't uniform throughout the league. It destroys data.

Experience of the referees vary as does confidence and often the lesser experienced referees are working the western conference. How does that affect analytics? It surely does because it's a part of the game where there actually is an ability to score on a power play. And just like hockey players, referees can be subjected to travel fatigue. It's a pretty natural thing to see referees, as professional as they may be, let things go on the last game of their road trip because they want to get on a plane as soon as possible and head home. Now it's doubtful anyone consciously says that or does that but the body fatigues, you can get into a rhythm just like any other job and think things are going great and you let it go and let it go and then the game is over and maybe the next day you review your job performance and realize it wasn't going as good as you thought. This is pretty common with almost every profession from truck drivers to fishermen to piloting. Sleep is super important.

Teams that travel on the west coast are pretty obviously getting less sleep than those in the Eastern Conference even with wonderful chartered airplanes and pre-custom clearances they're still having to be awake to get on the plane, get off the plane, get through customs, get through the airport, get in the car, get home, unwind, get some sleep. And so analytics can't tell you, in a physical game such as hockey, what you're seeing on the ice through simple data. It's harder to be a player, coach or general manager in the Western Conference than it is to be one in the Eastern Conference.

If you simply look at the Calder Trophy winners you can see the disparity between East and West. The kids learning on the west coast are at a huge disadvantage. If you simply look at the Vancouver Canucks as an example you could say they do a terrible job of drafting and developing hockey players. But then if you really look at it where else would it be more difficult to try and play in the NHL? It makes you wonder how good someone like a Trevor Linden could have been or how good Pavel Bure really was. And as previously stated, playing in a dead puck era.

If you're in a division with heavy teams the physical battering you're going to take is going to be different than a team playing in the old North Eastern Division for example (changed to Atlantic.) And so what data you're getting from analytics is probably a false positive depending on what you're looking at and what division the player is in. In football you can expect the same level of physicality from game to game. It is, by its very nature, a physical game. Punishing the opponent is the objective. But in hockey the size of the opponents and their physicality varies from team to team, division to division.

In the salary cap era of course you can't stack talent and you have massive variations from year to year and if you're seeing massive variations at the top level (only one Stanley Cup repeat in two decades) then it goes without saying, or should go without saying, that nothing below the top level can be accurately measured. The league is in constant flux and so the game itself is based on a level of chaos and the league is also experiencing chaos from year to year.

One other aspect of analytics which causes it to be less than useful is injuries. Who is playing with whom? Not all players are created equal. So if a third pairing defenseman loses his partner now he's into a number seven guy on the depth chart playing with him who might not be the right hand and is not suited to his style of play. A team with a lot of injuries, such as the Vancouver Canucks in 2016/17 with over 400 man games lost due to injuries, is using a 12th guy on the depth chart on the blue line and an 8th guy with an entirely new third and fourth lines. Well, there's no way anybody's "possession" numbers are going to look good, is there? They're in "all hands on deck" mode which means scramble, scrap, compete and forget the systems. Just do the best you can. And of course it affects the team they're playing, right? The Canucks injuries started on day one, so you never really got a read on who they were. It's pretty much true of any team at the bottom of the standings. You're going to see a ton of people on the injured reserve list. So at what point does the injured reserve list factor into your assessment of players using statistics? Well, I would argue after one injury you can toss the statistics out. It's a team game and now you're short-handed.

And then of course, how do you factor in less talented teams and how a player is affected by nobody on the ice able to help him? Or playing in the wrong role? But trying damned hard. If a player is playing for a 30th place team he's going to look really bad but then if he goes to a top contender all of a sudden, what do you know? The guy can play a lot better than statistically he should be playing. An example of this is Scott MacLeod in 2017 going from the Colorado Avalanche, 30th, and being traded to the Nashville Predators and becoming an integral part of the Predators lineup by being physical all the way to the Stanley Cup Finals.

Analytic nerds fail to remember hockey is a physical game. You'll often hear "why is so-and-so playing on the top line?" over and over again. His possession numbers are awful. He doesn't score goals. Jayson Megna for the Vancouver Canucks was often lamented by the media as a horrible hockey player and they were downright angry that he was on the ice on power plays. They failed to realize the guy was a physical presence without doing any of that statistically. He continued to work through check after check to get after the puck. And while he didn't paste a lot of people to the boards or fight often he never stopped competing. How do you put a grade on competing? You need guys like that on a team who don't do a lot with the fancy stats but who lead the way competing at 100% every game. It also shows you what coaches want, guys with maybe limited talent who skate fast and compete really hard and are good in their own zone. I'm going to contradict myself a little bit by saying you do, in fact, need one or two of these guys on your team by all means. But just not a whole team of hard working plumbers which is what you have now at the NHL for the most part.

Courage can't be measured. It is possible to tell who has the courage to get over the boards when games get physical and some players really excel at it. So what is the association between the physical level of the game and the desire of the players to get over the boards and get involved? Which player really loves it? Which one genuinely is having a good time fighting, spearing, cross-checking and enjoying all of the physical aspects hockey has to offer a young man or woman?

When you get into this analytic stuff, it's often forgotten that fighting is allowed in hockey. It's a necessary part of the game to make more room for yourself or others by casting a bigger shadow as someone who's got a short fuse and if you check them they might drop the stick and gloves and all of a sudden you're in a fight you weren't expecting. All hockey players need a certain amount of courage just to get on the ice. To really excel at the game you need to be like a Montreal Canadiens' Maurice Richard with a quick temper on the ice and a gentleman off the ice.

If you look solely at analytics you can miss the courage of hockey players. Another Canucks example is an Alexander Burrows. He was never drafted. He thought he was going to eke out a living in the East Coast Hockey League. But his compete level was off the chart and as it turned out his talent level was ridiculously high. He had 35 goals and 35 assists in his draft year along with 184 penalty minutes. I don't know how you could miss the 184 PIMs from a fairly small guy. It's completely baffling how no one saw Burrows loved competing and you didn't need fancy stats to see it because he was right there in the penalty box bleeding for everyone to see. That dog could hunt. If he was a second or third line player and had those statistics then it should have screamed NHL to anyone looking. Being physical matters and it's not necessarily fighting. It's that short temper.

Analytics doesn't see the player who gets slashed then grits his teeth in a snarl, turns around and spears him back. Hockey is eliminating these players because maybe they don't fit in the conventional box of fancy stats numbers. In my opinion it's stupid because compete can take care of a lot of things. A perfect example of this is the New England Patriots. Yeah, maybe they have a great quarterback, but people forget he competes at a level no one else does and was a late round pick. You often see Brady gritting his teeth and yelling at his own players and the opposition. The Patriots draft players based on compete levels and not strictly on how fast they are in a 40 yard dash. It's the same thing in hockey but accentuated because fighting is allowed. It's all fine and dandy to be a great little puck mover but does he grit his teeth when slashed and lose his mind in fury? That's what analytics doesn't show you and that's winners. And winners are mean sons of bitches without exception.

So there's very little to be gleamed from analytics. It would be like looking out the window of a space shuttle as it is achieving orbit and saying, ahhh, that's what the planet Earth looks like. Yes and no. Yes, it does look like that, if you're flying upwards at 15,000 miles per hour and looking out a window on a space shuttle while everything is violently shaking. It's interesting. It's neat. But it's a snapshot and not a wide perspective. It's useful if you like to look out a window of something moving 15,000 miles per hour, but what you would find is that it's difficult for the eyes and the brain to comprehend no matter how many times the scenario is repeated. You couldn't use that window as a way to start analyzing planet Earth.

If analytics continues to stress "possession" of the puck and pressures the loss of the physical game, especially in junior, then the NHL will continue to suffer. What will happen is the continuation of drone hockey players or entire teams of worker bees. While teams do need some drones you need a complete roster of every type of player to create an exciting hockey team.

FIXING THE DRAFT

In 1977 Ken Linseman launched a lawsuit against the NHL challenging the ban on drafting underage hockey players (under 20 years of age) which had been established in 1963 when the draft started. He had argued, fairly, that he had the right to work at 18. Linseman later dropped the lawsuit but it opened the door to the NHL drafting 18-year-olds because having a 20-year-old draft would need to be part of the collectively bargained agreement or CBA. The affect of this change would start impacting, logically, players entering the system at the age of five or so and then being drafted at the age of 17 but turning 18 in that draft year by September. So in 1990, 13 years after 1977, you would start seeing the impact. And sure enough that's what happened. (Thirteen because people put their kids into hockey at four or five.)

Boys aren't finished growing at 18 yet they're being evaluated at the age of 17 for the draft. The chances of teams getting the pick right become a lottery soon after the top two picks because there's so much uncertainty drafting such young people. And it puts enormous pressure on minor hockey kids and it shouldn't and it leads to all kinds of problems and a bad NHL product.

One of the best ways to get better at anything is to play older and more experienced or stronger players. You tend to learn in an awful hurry if you're 18 and playing against 20-year-olds. Today kids enter Canadian Junior hockey at 15 and they can be finished their junior career at 17 if they make the NHL at 18. In a 20-year-old draft by the time the same player is 18 he's going to be a much more complete and mature prospect with two more years of development left rather than someone who is playing two years against kids.

So what an older draft does is allow more time for younger players to develop before they hit the meat grinder of junior hockey. Currently Major Junior has 20-year-olds but restricted numbers instead of an entire team. Now NHL teams are evaluating boys, not men. If the NHL drafted at 20, as they used to, they can see clearly because their potential draft pick is playing against other men and not 15-year-olds (which currently happens.) It's more likely that these athletes are going to develop somewhere between the age of 18 and 20 rather than 16 and 18. So when you draft at 20 you're getting a finished product.

Currently the Canadian Hockey League (Major Junior level) only allows three 20-year-olds. If you allowed a 20-year-old draft you're going to see teams with more than half of their team loaded with 20-year-olds and the rest will be 19. The competition level is going to go through the roof. The vast majority of the team would be 20, with a few 19-year-olds and the odd 18-year-old. Those 17 and 18-year-old kids will now be looking for a place to play while waiting for a spot in major junior. This opens up Junior A, Tier II and Junior B hockey to a whole new level of talent influx. And that's really good because it feeds universities and NCAA colleges (you can't play Major Junior and enter the NCAA) because they accept kids at 18. Now education becomes a real avenue in case the NHL dreams don't work out. You can see talented youngsters going to college in their community and playing junior hockey for a few bucks to pay for tuition. But it definitely means completing high-school from Grade 8 to 12 where they started and with their friends.

It also means an explosion of something that disappeared - juvenile hockey leagues. Juvenile hockey divisions were extremely important for several reasons. First off it lets young impressionable kids go into arenas and see actual 18 and 19-year-old boys they probably know playing in front of them. And don't think for one second that isn't important. This is where they're going to have the most impact on young children not at junior levels with people in stands screaming and yelling but in the small hometown rink watching an older brother or a friend actually playing on the ice and realizing, hey, I can do that too. It's a really big deal. It's easy to forget how Grade 6 kids idolize those Grade 12s. They're a really big deal. And it's a really big deal for the grade 12s to see the little guys watching them play hockey. It matters.

Juvenile hockey is for 17 to 19-year-olds who want to finish high-school in their own town with their friends and who have either played rep or house and may or may not think of being drafted into Major Junior but might want to pursue a hockey career. That's super important. Some kids need an extra year in school. Some are late entering into kindergarten or for whatever reason it's an extra place for older kids to play who may in fact catch the hockey bug at 15 and want somewhere to play beyond 16 and 17 when midget is over. It's so important to catch these late bloomers and juvenile hockey is the answer. Juvenile becomes the new Midget. Juvenile is where the Major Junior leagues are going to scout along with Midget hockey. And that's appropriate.

Without question the biggest problem of a 18-year-old draft is that in many cases parents have to let their sons leave home at 15. I'll just repeat that because it is 2017 and not 1932, kids entering Major Junior are as young as 15. It means people are being selected for junior hockey at 14. So the cutoff for hockey, believe it or not, is a ridiculous 14 years of age. The cutoff used to be 17 years of age but because everything got rolled back now you have serious problems with a lot of things. So at the age of 14 moms and dads have to make tough decisions to push their children out of the home. And in some cases parents put their children into hockey schools as young as 14 such as Notre Dame Hounds program in Saskatoon where they specialize in a hockey program. Two examples from my neck of the woods would be William Mitchell and Rod Brind'amour. It's a really difficult decision for parents to make and Saskatoon is a long, long ways from Vancouver Island. I remember speaking to Rod Brind'amour's dad about this and he said it was very tough but Rod wanted to do it. And he said, Rod wasn't noticeably better than the other kids but you go to these schools and get really good. But at the age of 14 or 15 they're out the door. That's tough.

So what the 18-year-old draft has done is accelerate childhood and it can be really dangerous. Former Calgary Flames star forward Theo Fleury could testify about the dependency on a predator pedophile coach such as Graham James. They're not really old enough to leave home and stand up for themselves at that age and they can become victimized by predators who hold power over them.

I've always found it odd that the Canadian government hasn't stepped in and pressured the NHL and NHLPA back to the negotiating table to work out a 20-year-old draft where it should be set just for safety purposes. And really I'm surprised no one has gone to court to get immediate action. Nobody should have to let their little fella leave home at 15. I also need to point out that Graham James is the exception and not the rule; and there are benefits to letting children be parented by someone else. But I have a 15-year-old daughter and she's not leaving home until she's 32. (I'm kidding. 40.)

There's no way in hell I would allow my kids to leave my sight at 15 and I think the vast majority of parents are like myself. I think it would be fantastic if hockey programs were finishing schools for 17 to 19-year-olds instead of 14 and up. To me that makes a ton of sense. At grade 12 I think you're ready for your child to have an experience and what better one than going to a hockey program and trying to make the NHL? I love that idea. But 14 is way too young.

You're pressurizing the crockpot with an 18-year-old draft. Let me explain. You have all these kids in the hopper at the age of 12. And you don't want to lose them. But at the age of 13 they have to make a decision to play rep hockey (top tier of hockey) so that they can get drafted for junior at 14 and leave home at 15. So in those two years you have complete insanity. I can't tell you the number of tremendous hockey players I saw growing up who could have easily played junior, and a lot did later on - after age 15. But they were already behind the eight ball and didn't make it to the NHL because others had started so early. There were a lot of kids whose parents withheld them or discouraged progression instead putting their kids in other sports or a house league. So what you have is the real parental fear: "Oh my God, my child is good at hockey, how do I stop this?" That's contrary to getting talent into the NHL.

And for those parents who do push forward with the NHL dream and obviously don't make it what happens to them afterwards? Their kids missed out on a childhood because they started going for it at the age of five so what happens to them then? Is it a life full of regrets? I don't know. I can't find any studies about the failures. Do they have good lives afterwards? I think it's worthwhile for some psychology student to make this a study field and talk to these kids who don't make it 10 years afterwards. And talk to the parents too. Would they have done it again? Did they regret spending so much effort in forcing children to do something instead of enjoying the moment? Was it really worth it?

It takes a particular type of parent who is bound and determined for the child to make it to push them into something like that knowing, presumably, the risk if it doesn't work out. I'm not casting judgement either. I don't presume these are bad people. It's just a parenting style I'm not comfortable with and I think the majority of the population isn't comfortable with. You have to be more driven than your child. You have to want it more than they want it in most cases. That's a really dangerous area to be in as a parent.

I remember walking into the rink one day with a long-time NHL player and his dad on the ice (the NHLer was about eight or nine) and his dad was yelling at him and the future NHLer was crying with tears rolling down his cheeks. I remember that as clear as day. It stuck with me. Now, I don't for one second think his dad was a bad person for yelling at his son and making him cry. But that scene was pretty intense. It was a different era too. Getting the threat of the belt from your dad wasn't uncommon for any of us. It's a bygone time. But I just remember thinking what was his dad doing on the ice in his hockey gear with his son? And then yelling at him? It did not look like a lot of fun. My dad never said a word to us about hockey other than good game or a chuckle. I never made it to the NHL and that kid did and he has millions of dollars and I don't so maybe it worked. But I always felt sorry for him all the years I watched him in the league.

And so in these frantic two years where these young guys are hitting puberty at different times, which is enough all by itself, you have these driven parents pushing their children and spending insane amounts of money on ice time, hockey schools, and rep teams all in the hopes their little Johnny is going to make the NHL. For some people money is everything and perhaps they have dollar bills in their eyes and not loved ones. For others perhaps the motivation is to push their son because they were pushed by their dad and that's how you make strong sons. Whatever the motivation behind this behaviour is it mirrors what you see with beauty queen daughters pushed into pageants at the age of five. And so you can imagine all of these pushing parents gathered in one arena with junior hockey scouts to watch these high drama games of 13-year-olds playing on a bantam rep team with everyone jockeying for position, ice time, coach lobbying and referee baiting. It's intense and it's completely insane.

The 20-year-old draft pushes all of that forward two years and further and in fact, much like the NCAA route in the USA, they can even enter Major Junior at 18. How would they get into junior if they missed the draft at 17? They simply start playing on juvenile house hockey leagues at 17 proving they can play against 20-year-olds but not having to leave home except for road trips. They can play midget rep hockey right up to 17 pretty much from mom's basement and they don't have to feel like they've missed the NHL because they haven't.

And so when other kids in high-school are talking to counsellors about what vocational school or university or college they're going to these kids can have scouts come in to the high-schools and talk to them about their junior hockey programs. Everything is as it should be in life.

Instead right now you're trying to accelerate a hockey program when boys are learning all sorts of other things besides hockey like girls, algebra, programming, girls, cars, friends and girls. So what's the end result? A ton of drop off from hockey at exactly the wrong age. Contrary to popular belief it's not the kids who learn to skate at the age of two who begin to excel at hockey. Wrong, wrong and more wrong. It's the kids who play every single sport available to them. They don't burnout.

It's not the hockey prodigy you want it's the athlete you want and most of them aren't getting serious about any sport until maybe the age of 12 and even then probably just dipping their toes in it. They play everything. These kids are catching sunrays off wet tennis balls and enjoying the loud smack as it hits a house. They're outside skipping rope, playing hopscotch (yes boys,) they're using peashooters to hit birds (I know that's bad but they're boys,) they're shooting pellet guns and then real guns, they're fishing every weekend with dad, they're swimming with friends, they're outside horsing around getting into fights for no reason they can remember. These are the kids you want playing hockey because unlike kids who specialize at a young age these kids are soaking everything in.

But what are they really doing? These kids are learning invaluable lessons about physics and geometry that must be learned before you can play hockey. What happens when I bounce a ball here? No matter what age you start hockey the space is finite. Geometry and physics are integral parts of hockey as is strength and force. Those are the lessons which later on translate to being a true master of the game. They need eyesight developed along a gun barrel or a slingshot. Throwing things. Breaking things. The thrill of getting in trouble and running for your life and seeing what fear is really like with lungs burning and legs stinging. These are your athletes.

The problem with centralizing all a child's training into one genre means the rest of the food group doesn't arrive at the NHL. They're specializing in hockey at such an early age to keep up with the Joneses that all of the kids are arriving at the same destination with exactly the same set of skills scouts are looking for at the peril of a Burrows or Robitaille. There's always more than one way to skin a cat. Right now everyone skates the same, handles the puck the same and is doing the same thing on the ice mainly because the scouting and hockey development process has been bottlenecked into the same area. The draft age of 18 exasperates the issue as everyone stampedes their children into the same hockey training. They all get to know each other and it becomes very difficult for outsiders to breakthrough. It's completely unnecessary and unhelpful if you wish to achieve a higher level of hockey.

I've heard hockey great Bobby Orr say that kids shouldn't even be playing rep hockey until the age of 10 that they play too many games nowadays. The Sedins have said virtually the same thing by saying that in Sweden you don't really start specializing in a sport until 12 or 13 and they look at our hockey system in amazement (I think probably they have a different word in mind.) It's incredibly stupid this amplifying of the intensity at such an early age. Rep hockey under the age of 14 is incredibly stupid because the kids aren't ready.

So many of these athletes would develop into the NHL's greats but this early stampede eliminates the creative, the gifted and the aloof. From being around the school system for four decades it's my experience artistic children can't be herded like cattle and prodded with a stick. They will rebel and they will leave the program flat out. They have no use for you and your stupid rules and restrictions. They will come to you. They're interested in studying the game and playing and learning at their own pace.

So what are you getting here because of the draft age at 18? You're getting basically kids that can handle the Marine Corps at 13 or 14. It's going to be exactly the same player succeeding over and over again. The artistic children are not going to wear suits at 12. They couldn't care less about making the cut. Those are the kids that end up being the terrific hockey players. They think independently and don't want the stench of conforming all over them. They're more likely to give such a military style program the middle finger and walk.

And what about those kids who have hit puberty later? Or not as strongly as other kids? The hockey changing room is a very spartan and harsh environment for young kids. There's usually no private changing area. There's no private showers. It's a cement block with one door and people coming in and out. It's more like a prison bathroom than anything else. If you're a sensitive boy it's going to remove you from the picture because of the fear of ridicule. And it's these sensitive kids that are usually artistic and soak everything in like a sponge. Not all, I admit that's a generalization.

But what I'm saying is that a draft age of 20 maximizes the numbers of children moving forward in hockey and doesn't cull the herd before the beef is ready for market. The Washington Post story on June 1, 2016, entitled "Why 70 percent of kids quit sport by 13" captures the essence of the argument. "It's not fun anymore because it's not designed to be," says Julianna Miner in her article. Scores start mattering more than fun. Stats start to matter. Parents start to ratchet up the intensity of cheering. It becomes stupid at some point. And so kids starting to exercise their independence walk away from the sport.

And as previously touched on the obvious thing about the 18-year-old draft is you have NHL scouts trying to evaluate 17-year-olds. They spend a year following around a 17-year-old child. It would be something out of a Monty Python skit except it's real. You see the same thing happening in the NBA when it started to draft freshman. The games got worse. They're not ready at these young ages. There might be a couple of players who are ready to step in but if they had been allowed to develop a couple more years, such as an Auston Matthews of the Toronto Maple Leafs, you might really have someone who can dominate in all facets of the game. Unfortunately Matthews is as likely to disappear in the coming years as get better because he was in the league too early and so the consistency disappears.

You get a lot of "flash in the pan" top draft picks who arrive and disappear and that's a death sentence for a league dependent on first round draft picks more than any other league. Edmonton Oilers centre Connor McDavid had a terrific season in 2016/17 but couldn't scratch 40 goals. None of them can get to 50. They come into the league almost ready but not quite as evident by their flameouts in the playoffs to mediocre teams.

Four to five years after the draft you can look back and say this player selected at 4th overall was a mistake and this one, taken at 33rd overall, was a Hall of Famer. It's almost completely random. So with every scout pouring over the pool of 17-year-olds they all look for the same thing and that's speed because it's measurable. So the other talents come second. And what you end up with at the NHL are a whole bunch of people who play exactly the same way. Strength on skates is as important as speed and can nullify checking. The ability to move laterally, to shift speeds, to avoid checks is as equal to pure speed but it's not drafted anymore.

Speed became the end all to be all in the draft process forgetting slower players have more time to assess things. Speed is not everything or it shouldn't be everything in a sport with boards. And given how NHL franchises hang in the balance of these kids there isn't any room for a mistake. It's an impossible task at these young ages. Someone who is ranked 25th in a draft at 18 could easily overtake the first overall pick by age 23 and you see it all the time. It's virtually impossible for scouts to assess these kids projecting forward to the age of 23. It would be so much more accurate if they were looking at 20-year-olds because obviously you're seeing closer to the real thing.

The best way to maximize your chances for success in the draft is to simply take the fastest skaters with the best goal scoring ability and work your way downwards. Skating faster in a finite space doesn't create opportunity. It shortens the ability to make advantages. Mario Lemieux would skate over the blue line and stop. And then he would stick handle, while standing there, past anyone who tried to take the puck away. And often he would vary his speed when on the attack. It was almost always different and very hard for a defender to read him. He was the quarterback on the ice surveying the field for an opportunity.

Speed only helps defensively by closing the gap quicker but for someone who knew what they were doing it could also be used against them by anticipating they're going to speed rush. Jaromir Jagr would just turn his butt into them and use his backhand to dish the puck off. It's only limited by imagination. But because of the 18-year-old draft you're eliminating the artist too early and then you're forcing these kids to learn on the job. It's a closed loop system and feeding it just speed can only produce what you're seeing right now which is drone hockey.

Variety is the spice of life. Gone are the kids who were one dimensional passers working with pure shooters and a tough guy. As the vortex towards the draft increases, more and more of the kids who learn to be exceptional at one area of the game are excluded. All of the kids today are pumped into factories teaching them to skate this way, shoot this way, be here when this happens, and you get a formulaic hockey result. Many kids used to learn the advantages of goal sucking or dogging it on the back check looking for a turnover. One of the best ways of scoring goals is to not rush back into your own zone and stand in front of your net but to hang out behind the play giving a teammate an opportunity to spring them for a breakaway or turnover. A lot of these players have learned the game from a different angle. They base it on hunches and intuition and they really don't need to be able to skate like an Olympian speed skater. In fact the slower they go the more room they're giving themselves. But of course it leaves only four guys back in their own zone laying on the ice in front of their goaltender. Even if they turned the puck over it's unlikely a teammate could pass them the puck because they're usually laying prone on the ice. It's a waste of time.

So what succeeds in the draft are players who can skate like the dickens back into their own zone and stand in front of their own net blocking shots. You often hear "we can teach them that" on draft day, referring to defensive hockey but what you will never hear is someone saying, "I think we can teach him to score at the NHL level." Defense is the priority even for so-called offensive players.

If they were allowed to develop a little longer, scouts would be more confident in knowing what they were drafting and then you could draft by position instead of "best talent available" which doesn't help anyone. Can you imagine the laughter if that was said at the NFL in the first round of their draft? They choose by positional need knowing these kids, most at 21, are ready to step right in and play.

The NHL used to be like the NFL. You could pretty much count on what you were drafting. The problem with the way it's working now is not just that teams can languish for 10 or more years in the bottom of the league it's also that after the 10 years of waiting for a franchise player only to find out their whiz kid isn't quite ready to help and furthermore they have only marginal hockey players to surround him on the ice. Even if you get one of these players you quickly find out they can't maximize their impact because everyone else is playing exactly the same way. There isn't a division of talent anymore. They all come from the same cookie-cutter way which is skate as fast as you can.

Also there's the physiology to consider of a 17-year-old. They're about four years away from being finished growing. So you can draft 6'2" and 150 pound players and hope they will grow into their bodies. But what if they don't? At 21 if that player is still 180 pounds then they are what is called slight and it's not ever going to change. So you have the absurdity of scouts looking at parents and grandparents and trying to decipher genetics and make a guess as to whether someone will end up at 210 pounds instead of 180 pounds.

And then there's the guessing whether someone will mesh with the collection of other players from around the world. How will the Swede with skill fit into the game of Red Rover with the team of Canadian plumbers? It's fairly random and so you end up with teams that just never get out of the development hole no matter how long they stay at the bottom of the draft. And the only teams that win the Stanley Cup are ones that get lucky drafting a couple of very good players which happens every six or seven years. It's pretty rare the cycle is broken. And this will get worse as the league becomes 32 teams with less talent to draw from and players who just aren't ready to play.

This leads to a problem of instability in ownership as well because people buy an NHL team thinking it will take five to seven years to build a winner but soon find out it will take 20 years just to get competitive, never mind winning a Stanley Cup which is dependent on drafting luck. And so they quit and try to sell the team and there isn't another owner available for some time such as the Arizona Coyotes where the league had to finance the team through a series of owners.

But the common thread of this is the unpredictability of the draft. The kids are generally five years away from being effective hockey players and at best their first round draft picks are 25 goal scorers which isn't helping anyone. Even Connor McDavid barely crested 30 goals. Goals matter. Goals are everything and when you used to get kids in the draft routinely scoring 100 goals in junior hockey and that would translate to being a 40 goal scorer at the NHL now you're hoping for a 30 goal scoring junior to develop into a 15 goal scorer at the NHL level. That's how bad it has become. Scouts are drooling over junior hockey players with 30 goals and calling that an "extremely talented goal scorer." It's no wonder these kids come up and can't score goals because they've never breached 50 goals in any previous level. How on Earth would they be expected to do it at the highest level?

And what if a player drafted at 18 is too good for junior but can't make the NHL? They have to go back to junior because they're not allowed to go to the AHL and play for the NHL's farm team. They have to be 20 to get into the AHL (with some exceptions). And so they can waste two years after being drafted not getting any better playing against 17-year-olds.

The other weird thing about an 18-year-old draft is that these players start to get agents talking to them at 15. If you think about that for a second you realize how messed up the system is. These kids can't buy a beer, they can't drive a car, but they have a guy in a suit and tie talking about contracts and best moves for careers. I understand this also happens in the other sports but it still doesn't make it right. What have we done? We've turned growing up into a pressure cooker that rewards parents who take massive risks with their children, as well meaning as they might be. Sidney Crosby had a personal trainer at 10 and was under a hockey workout regimen at 14. I don't know the family or Crosby at all but I can say it sets off my parent alarm. They're probably loving parents and wanted the best for Crosby. But to me as a parent I could never push my child at such a young age. It's just putting expectations on a child that I don't want anywhere near them until they're 18.

I do understand that exercise is a good thing for kids and certainly Crosby would have benefitted. And you should push children to some extent. But where is the line now? Personal trainers? Who has that kind of money to spend on a child? And what happens to those kids that don't make it? For every Crosby there must be hundreds of failed "child prodigies."

The government does all kinds of studies on everything under the sun but we don't take a look at something which is potentially as harmful as our current minor hockey systems. We should be looking and if necessary taking steps to prevent parents from going too far. It's starting to get into communist area where you select kids that show athletic promise and push them in athletics and only athletics eight hours per day. If it turns out, great. If it doesn't though, you could have a whole host of problems on your hands. Clearly the NHL and NHLPA need to bargain a 20-year-old draft similar to the best league in the world the NFL. And the government of Canada should intervene to let the NHL know it would be in their best interests to do so and it needs to start looking into what's going on in the race to make it to the NHL.

BALL, STREET OR FLOOR HOCKEY

One of the significant downfalls of hockey is the collapse of street hockey in rural and suburban Canada. You just don't see anyone playing road hockey anymore. On the way home from the grocery store today before writing this chapter, I passed four boys in two sets with a basketball in their hands bouncing it on the sidewalk presumably on a way to shooting hoops. I haven't seen a game of road hockey in years or kids going anywhere with a stick in their hands. And in this city there are a couple of dedicated areas for ball hockey. They're talking about plowing them under because no one uses them.

Ball hockey whether it's on the street or in a gym (floor) is the best place to learn to play hockey because ice hockey is really two different games. Hockey is one game by itself and so is skating. And anyone can play road hockey. There's no large amount of money required. But unfortunately there's no leadership from the top, such as Hockey Canada or the NHL, to make sure road hockey is a vibrant part of the culture. It seems there is only interest in ice hockey which really can't exist without road hockey providing the players for its system. There are ball hockey leagues in larger urban areas, which is fantastic, but it doesn't get to the kids who can combine the ball or road hockey into ice hockey. (The demand for ice rinks in large urban areas is too extreme to produce hockey players unless their parents can send them to a place such as Burnaby Winter Club hockey academy, in a suburb of Vancouver.)

There are a few other sports on the planet incorporating two different games like hockey such as water volleyball which incorporates swimming and volleyball. Both disciplines need to be learned before they can be melded together. In hockey right now what you have is an almost exclusive learning of the game of skating. There's only so much time in the day for these kids. They are pushed and pulled in a lot of directions by computers, video games, smart phones, television, school and life and they're restricted in the ability to go outside and hang out. The best way to learn hockey is to play street hockey from sunrise to sunset on weekends and after school.

Kids are being pushed into skating and hockey year round today. And when they're not skating they are in the gym. Part of the reason is they're in a supervised area where kids are fairly safe. And so what happens is that the kids get less practice playing hockey.

Road hockey is by far superior to ice hockey when learning the game. It teaches you pace because you can't run up and down the road or tennis court like you can an ice sheet with skates. What happens is the kids learn to move the puck more than their feet. They learn the art of standing still and ball handling to buy time. No one would play the game of hockey itself the way they play at the NHL level which is running up and down the court as fast as you can in 30 second bursts. And again, anyone can play ball hockey because there's little cost involved.

Street or ball hockey could and should be developed as an Olympic sport because everyone can play it on any continent. You don't need ice and skates. All you need are shoes, a stick and a tennis ball and somewhere to play. The fact it's in decline, at least in this neck of the woods, is contributing to the lack of talent at the NHL.

It's always good to look at any game and see how far from its roots it has travelled to determine its health. Football developed from rugby and created the forward pass. Other than that it's pretty much the same game year after year. Basketball added a three point circle but has kept Mr. Naismith's original plan intact. Baseball added the designated hitter but has remained pretty much the same for 125 years. But hockey has significantly changed from the forward pass, to the number of players to continual tinkering with the game. It's to the point where street hockey and ice hockey have diverged as separate sports. That's a really bad thing since it is road hockey which provides the talented hockey players in ice hockey. Ball or road hockey provides the pure game of hockey without complicating it with skating. You can see the game from a steady platform.

Road hockey is where the stars are born. These are the kids who spend hours and hours a week smacking the tennis ball into a garage door to see how it bounces back and to improve wrist shot, snap shot, slap shot, backhand. And they play with their curves by heating their super blades (rubber stick blades that you can attach to a handle) in boiling water on the kitchen stove or using a propane torch or however they do it. It's the bouncing the ball off trees and fences and cars and determining weights and angles that give the special hockey players their love of the game. It's solving the mystery of what happens if I do this? They continually experiment with angles alone and in games until it's second nature to them. And they try with orange hard balls, tennis balls, pucks and soccer balls - whatever they can find, and see how it reacts when struck. These are the kids who fall in love with the game. These are the ones that learn shinny, a scramble hockey where every one is a forward and everyone is a defenseman and everyone takes a turn in net. And they play until their lungs hurt and then push a little more forcing their bodies to become stronger and stronger until they develop a form of surfer knee. The main thing about road hockey is the price. It's almost free aside from a tennis ball and an old wooden hockey stick. Nets can be two rocks or whatever they can find.

With the pushing of specialization into ice hockey at the exclusion of all other sports, kids don't learn the game the way they used to learn it. They never get a summer off to learn to play hockey or basketball, lacrosse, football or whatever it is that tickles their fancy. Hockey is the one game where you can take everything from every sport and put it all together. If you play quarterback in football then you can take that into hockey, surveying the field looking downwards for a pass either a home run pass or short dump off. If you play baseball then you learn the art of deflecting 80 mph fastballs and you can translate it on the ice into deflecting slapshots or wrist shots. A hockey player is the one athlete who can stop on any field or court and play the game no matter what it is. I guarantee they can do it because of the hockey background. Conversely, the other athletes couldn't play hockey. So it's a very complicated game to master. Disruptions in the practice times have grave affects on players. The rushing of 12-year-olds into the pro ranks casts aside the most important training ground which is the front street.

Canada has changed since the 1950s, obviously, along with the rest of the world. Parents don't like to leave their kids unattended for long. And it's completely understandable with the advent of serial child killers and television broadcasting the dangers of parenting daily. No one wants to take the risk of losing their child or getting reported to social services for neglect of a child by letting them play from dusk to dawn outside.

My generation of parents would tell the kids to go outside after breakfast and they really didn't care too much where we went. We were outside except for dinner or lunch breaks. Rain, sleet or sunshine it didn't matter. Parents don't have the luxury of outdoor parenting like that today. They also have to worry about crazy drivers. I grew up in a place where the grownups were very respectful of hockey games and were, in short, grownups. It isn't the case anymore for a variety of reasons.

Different cultures of people have immigrated to Canada with different values. They may not value driving slowly the way Canadians did for years. They come from time constraints and impatience on the road and so it's a bad mix to play street hockey where they drive (and that's not all newcomers and not all Canadians.) Now to be fair, we all have changed. Everyone drives faster and faster. Family cars used to be fairly slow compared to the vehicles on the road today which seem to urge drivers onwards to speed. There's nothing more dangerous on the road than a woman and her brand new 250 hp minivan (I'm sorry but that's my wife's saying, not mine. And it's true.) Some of them drive it like they stole it. And there's just more of us everywhere which causes congestion. Some municipalities have even banned road hockey to prevent serious accidents. Distracted driving didn't exist 30 years ago. Now you can catch someone on a smartphone pretty much every time you look at the car beside you at the next traffic light. They certainly could drive right into a street hockey game.

I grew up in a place where you could watch Ronald's mom warm the station wagon up for 5 minutes while she smoked a dart. And so you knew she was coming. And then she'd stop in the middle of the game to say out the fogged window, "Hey, Ronnie. I'm going to the grocery store." Can you imagine today if someone left their eight-year-old alone on a street to play hockey for 30 minutes?

Ball hockey is so important because it's all ages, all experience, both sexes, any number of players with any combination of numbers on the teams whether it's two adults verse 12 kids or seven on seven. This is really critical because it teaches kids all of the things they might experience in hockey for example what it's like to be on a three on nothing breakaway or defending against five. All of these weird combinations are thrown into the hopper in road hockey. It's completely random. There might be a pothole on the street that you can bounce the ball in or to be wary of. And a huge part of it is what happens when you miss a shot or make a bad pass or miss a bad pass because you're going to have to get the ball back and it might be 100 feet down the road or worse into a wet ditch or even worse, hit dog poo. And it might be uphill or downhill again teaching different angles and weights. So you'd better learn really quickly to take a pass or make that shot right on the money. Or you're running after a ball.

There comes a point in hockey where the game slows down. You see things before they happen. With the death of most street hockey there's fewer kids making it to this special point because it takes an extraordinary amount of time to get there. It's extremely expensive to get that amount of time at an arena so no one at the NHL level reaches the level before entering the NHL.

Some NHL players reach it in their late twenties. Joe Thornton has been at this very high level for the past 10 years. So have the Sedins. (Interestingly the Sedins credit soccer for most of their playmaking ability.) Crosby and Alexander Ovechkin are close but they bullrush more than they play the game. The best way to describe this level is that the hockey player does something truly beautiful on the ice. Crosby and Ovechkin really force the issue. They don't step out of the game. Perhaps that will come as they are both just 30.

Ball hockey is the best way to get to this next level. Because the game is slower on foot it allows for easier assimilation of the game and seeing the nuances and you don't have to worry about crashing into the boards or stopping or starting. Once you get older, around the age of 10, you can then take those lessons from street hockey and put it on the ice knowing what should be done. While these kids who have mainly played street hockey will be behind those kids, initially, who have paid a lot of money for ice skating, the tables will soon turn. Skating is just a means to an end. It's just a tool to get from point A to point B. Someone who has mainly played road hockey, and a lot of it, will instinctively know where to go and when to go as opposed to someone who has only played limited amounts of ice hockey.

There's so much going on in the game without complicating it with skating and drills. Skating is just a tool. That's all it is. It's a necessary evil to play the game. Once you start down the road of thinking this particular tool is the only tool you need then it only stands to reason the rest of the kid's game is going to suffer badly and you see it at the NHL level. Too often you see these kids skate themselves right into traffic. It's just a rush game with no thought to slowing down. These kids have clearly spent more time in the gym than playing hockey.

Slowing down is as effective or more effective than rushing around. Kids who play road hockey instinctively know this. You have to learn to take short cuts or you're going to get dog tired before the game has started. Skating is a complication. Skating should always come second to hockey and never first. It's easier to learn to shoot the ball or puck in shoes than it is skates. It's easier to learn to manipulate the stick when you're on solid footing. I think one of the reasons why USA hockey has bypassed Canadian hockey is because there is so much road hockey in the south including roller blading.

Another reason why the USA has passed Canada in talent development is the lack of a junior hockey program. The kids play high-school hockey there where they live while continuing to practice and play daily and it includes a lot of non-ice playing. Junior hockey requires meetings and travel and drills.

The following is a quote taken directly from the American Development Model, USA Hockey, web page ADMkids.com/about, right at the top.

What's wrong with where we're going?

For starters, many athletes spend too much time traveling, competing and recovering from competition and not enough time preparing for it. Second, there is too heavy a focus on the result rather than the performance. This attitude leads to long-term failure, as coaches forgo the development of skills to focus on specific game tactics. And third, too many athletes are specializing too early on. An early focus on just one or two sports often leads to injuries, burnout and capping athletic potential.

As a Canadian I admire the way Americans see the problem, identify the problem, fix the problem. They just have this attitude of not being afraid of anything. They roll their sleeves up and get it done. And that simple paragraph sums up my lengthy arguments to a T. "... capping athletic potential." Without question it's what you see at the NHL. You get players who are manufactured in a warehouse.

If you compare it to the Canadian Minor Hockey Association website you can't read the entire page because the "links" cover up the information. There's no mission statement at the front. It's really unwelcoming and unhelpful, to be frank. It also has training and selection mentioned multiple times on the first page. The "selecting a coach" is particularly unpleasant to me. Questions for the coach, how to select a coach, forms for players and parents to fill out. Umm, how about no? You're only going to get a certain type of person who likes to fill out forms and dance through hoops as a coach. I've known people in my life who couldn't read and yet were the smartest people I've ever met. And once you go down this form and selection stuff you're going to eliminate the people you want coaching - those who don't really want to do it. They are always the best coaches because they never get emotionally involved in it.

I go back to street hockey as the example of how best to develop kids in hockey. Playing against older people. As a young kid when you're out on the ice or the road or whatever it is you're doing you grow quickest playing against people twice your age. Learn quick or never touch the ball or puck. If you think about it, these are the adults you want coaching the guys who just grab a stick and get out and play on the street with the kids and give'r!

It's been my experience that these are likely to be the high-school dropouts or high-school graduates who have a trade and who really don't like paperwork, thus the not continuing to university aspect of their lives. What you have in Canada right now is a hockey system geared for book smart people. I've always learned more from men missing a tooth or finger than those with all of their digits. I don't know why that is for certain but it could be because they're really direct people. There's nothing hidden. And so what I'm saying by eliminating a lot of the development on the road for hockey you're steering all of these kids to upper middle-class university educated people, and, with all due respect, that's exactly the wrong people to teach hockey.

Hockey at its roots is still the game played by British soldiers on the ice in Eastern Canada. By that I mean the conscripts not the officers. Since its beginning as hurling over 3,000 years ago it's been a very rough sport and it has been for more than a century in Canada until recently where the salt of the Earth players started disappearing both from playing and coaching. Now you have lawyers and teachers and degrees and certificates and if you have enough money you can get your child into the NHL. True, someone like Pat Quinn had a law degree from prestigious Widener Law School of Delaware, earning it after he finished his career. Everyone benefits from an education I'm arguing for it. I'm talking about who players are before they get degrees and where they came from. They can't just come from large urban areas with money. It has to include sons of loggers, miners and farmers.

One of the biggest examples of the clashes of the old school players verses the new school of players can be seen in the Steve Moore / Marcus Naslund incident which occurred in February, 2004. Moore was Harvard educated before entering the NHL. Colorado's Moore hit the NHL's leading scorer, Naslund, squarely in the head. The later fight between Moore and Bertuzzi seemed like two different worlds colliding and the game changed after this because of the Harvard student's lawsuit. Moore seemed ill-prepared for the blood thirst he had unleashed from the old-school Bertuzzi. While wild incidents still continued they became quite infrequent. For example, in 2004 the Nashville Predators led the NHL with 79 fighting major penalties. By 2015 the Columbus Blue Jackets led the NHL with 44 fighting majors with most teams averaging around 30 fights per year.

I attribute this dramatic collapse of fighting to the streamlining of kids at an early age in Canada into a program taught and administered mainly by educated people and the increase of US college developed kids combined with the Steve Moore lawsuit chill. I believe since the NHL or NHLPA did not adequately defend Todd Bertuzzi in court and financially support him (paid any of his penalties) it altered the mindset of the people playing the game, naturally. I don't think anyone wants to be sued because it is an unpleasant experience and can lead to financial and professional ruin.

Hockey is no longer a simple game derived from ball hockey in many different ways. It is big business with huge investments in children. Now it's a game for those with parents who have deep pockets. And they don't need street hockey to get their kids into the NHL. They can buy development camps on ice. Those who used to play street hockey, who are still allowed to play street hockey, I guess have found no purpose for it because you rarely see it being played anymore. I mean, where is road hockey going to lead for these kids nowadays? They can't afford the ice hockey so then what? And it's such a shame because of its ties with hurling and the passion it injects into ice hockey. It is the changing of the game from passionate to dispassionate.

200 FOOT BY 85 FOOT PLAYING SURFACE

Hockey is a closed loop system more than any other sport because of a playing surface you can't leave. No other sport has the gladiator structure of hockey. Football and rugby are arguably more physical but hockey is by far the most violent and it's the closed playing surface which is the biggest factor (and a weapon in the hand.)

So if you have a closed loop system the faster you reach the end the faster you begin again. Some or all of the output is used in the input. What it means is that if you go faster it's going to end faster. Where are you going so fast? There's only 200 feet of playing surface. If you consider the scoring area is the 30 feet in front of the net to the net, then really you only have 170 feet. And if you're starting at the 40 foot mark, then it's 130 feet before you reach red zone. What's the rush to get there? It doesn't increase scoring opportunity it decreases time in the red zone or the slot. You can't score from the boards to about 15 feet out. So skating through the red zone to get to the boards isn't helpful and skating through the red zone even faster is less helpful. The objective is to get into the red zone and stay in the red zone until you can make a play either a shot or a pass closer to the net but not outside the red zone.

What you see nowadays is constant play outside the red zone because the opponents have stacked the "box" in front of the goalie. So what it requires is pinpoint passing to static stations in order to break the defense down. It doesn't require speed skating. What hasn't changed in hockey is the square footage an opponent uses on the ice meaning his stick blade and skate blades are the same size they were back in 1914. But what has happened is the players are moving faster both offensively and defensively thinking that in a closed loop system faster is better. But it isn't because the input feeds the output. Slowing down and passing the puck from point to point would actually allow more time for goal scoring. If you skate at 3/4 speed for example let's say it takes you 3 seconds to skate through the red zone. If you skate at full speed it takes you 1.5 seconds to get through the red zone. It's cut the opportunity in the red zone in half. But because kids are taught speed, speed, speed from the age of five this is what you see time and time again at the NHL level now without realizing it's not helpful.

Tony Esposito and Brad Park are two perfect examples of slowing down, even not moving, in the offensive zone and playing a pick and roll game like in basketball. Yes the players are faster today than Esposito. I would guess Sidney Crosby could skate from his blue line to 20 feet outside the opponent's net about one full second faster than Esposito (in his prime.) And so I'll pose the obvious question: So what? All it's done is remove about one second in the red zone from Crosby.

Now you may say, well, the defenseman is coming at Crosby so he has to go faster to get around him or to avoid him. Yes, absolutely that's true if you don't plan on beating the defenseman with a move. NHL players used to be able to stick handle in a phone booth; bent over, stick choked up, face three feet from the ice, butt swiveling around to the defenseman, buying time for someone to get open. The time it takes to close the gap between 1985 and 2015 is maybe half a second. That's all we're talking about. It's half a second faster but if you haven't learned the basic skills of keep away you're going to avoid doing it. What you're going to do is just skate and skate and skate around. And that's why you see what you see today. There are a few players who can still make magic out there such as the Blackhawk's American Patrick Kane, but he's almost unique in the NHL. I go back to the Mario Lemieux example of him standing just inside the blue line and putting the puck between a defenseman's skates, turning around through another defender and feeding a pass to a wide open Penguin beside the net. There was no panic from Lemieux.

Lemieux won a scoring title playing half a season coming back from cancer and when I heard media members suggesting after the 2017 NHL playoffs Crosby was even better than Lemieux I had to wonder what they were watching or were they even old enough to remember Lemieux playing? Crosby better than Lemieux actually came out of someone's mouth, multiple people's mouths in fact.

Lemieux scored in 75.4% of the games he played in or 690 goals in 915 games. Crosby is at a very respectable .488 percentage but he's not even in the Top 25 all time. He's not even close and that percentage will drop when he gets to the other side of 30. People who are involved in the game so deeply right now can't see the forest through the trees. I've yet to see Crosby do anything other than basic plays at the NHL level. Yes, he does these basic plays very fast, but there's never been a wow factor in Crosby's game. He's a great athlete and a decent hockey player but compared to Lemieux or Dionne? Oh gosh no. Not even close. You're talking about people who could make the puck sit up and sing during a game to people who skirt around the outside of the game and dart in and out of it through sheer hard work.

Faster hockey isn't better hockey. What got better with more speed? Anything? More concussions and violent injuries perhaps. The rink isn't getting bigger. It hinders offense. They're too busy skating to the corner with the puck. They haven't learned the basics of offense to start something in the slot because the game is going so quick even in practices.

Hits became more violent. Now hitting is leaving the game because if someone throws a decent hit everyone acts like it's the worst thing that has ever happened in the history of sports and inevitably there's a scrum, face washing and maybe a limited fight. And so there's less hitting in the game now because people don't want to have to fight afterwards and so when the physical play leaves the game then you just have speed skating.

The hip check also used to be common in the game but you might see it now two or three times per year for the entire league. Guys like Jiri Bubla of the Canucks and Rob Blake of the Los Angeles Kings made a living out of their backsides. It's completely gone from the game. It would be like the NFL removing flying tackles.

In a closed loop system the faster you go the easier it is to defend. You're getting to the boards quicker. You're avoiding the center of the ice. You've got boards. So options are limited. It favours the defender. A defenseman already knows the rushing forward is not going to do anything stupid at the blue line. I know you're going straight to the back of the net or the corners. I might as well just head there first and wait for you. And that's what happens. It's almost like a symphony out there with the tuba and clarinet players working in harmony.

As players got worse and the turnovers got more egregious could you blame the coaches for looking for a foolproof system? A lot of the kids nowadays handle the puck like it's a hand grenade. How many times do you see a defenseman whack the puck into the opponent's shin pads instead of making a move because it's the safe play? It's also the lazy play. It's just cashing in a paycheque. There's always an opportunity on every shot to get the puck through. The real estate the opponent is actually occupying on the ice hasn't changed in over 100 years. But finding players, particularly defenseman, who can exploit the on-rushing opponent is like finding a needle in a haystack today.

Even mediocre defenseman from 30 years ago would make a fortune in this current NHL because they almost all could get the puck on net without hitting an opponent. And the other thing they could do was whistle the puck at chin height. You almost never see a defenseman shoot the puck at an opponent's head anymore. Why did that play go away? Fear is a pretty good way to score a goal. If some idiot is going to rush at you to block a puck why aren't you making a point of a shot to the face? I'll put it another way. In baseball if pitchers continually let hitters crowd the plate they're going to launch home runs. So a pitcher absolutely has to throw inside and sometimes to make a point they have to throw chin music or even sometimes hit a player square in the back. You have to make a statement that this is about money and that's my plate get off of it. As that play has left MLB the home run totals have skyrocketed to record levels. Why don't you see head high shots in the NHL anymore? I'm just so shocked that power plays don't have defenseman launching about 10 shots head high to clear the net and buy time. You have to do it. You can't just concede the plate or in this case the net. The opponents don't have any fear in today's game of getting hurt because of the visors and the gear and the fact no one is trying to really hit them.

Road hockey kids learn pretty quickly that you can get space by showing you can whistle the puck eye level. In a 200 foot confined space if you concede the safety factor then you're virtually never going to score. It's meant to be a violent game. It's just not today. And while I appreciate the sportsmanship of not fighting, hitting or shooting at an opponent's head, the net result is a lack of excitement, entertainment and goals. And it's the latter that is easily provable.

Another result of chase hockey or Red Rover hockey is the increased time spent changing lines and not playing hockey. Think about it. You've got a confined space in a closed loop system. The human body only has a limited amount of endurance and when the player runs out of energy they have to change up by heading back to the bench for a new player to go on the ice.

I can't stress this enough as a main factor as to why scoring is down considerably. Line changes have become a significant time factor in the closed loop system.

Players used to conserve energy on the ice and go fast only when necessary. Line changes would happen at the whistles mainly and sometimes on the fly. But it wasn't uncommon for offensive players to be on the ice for a minute and a half. The norm now is 30 seconds. And so what happens now is the closed loop feedback hits the offensive player in the middle of an offensive drive. So often players have a chance to do something with some open ice and they get to centre ice and dump it in and return to the bench, literally turning the puck over, the very thing the coaches are yelling and screaming about. But that is called a good play even though they gave up the puck they got the puck deep and got "fresh" legs on the ice. But it just comes right back out because they went to the bench to change up. And because one player changes all five have to change.

Line changes used to involve about five percent of the game's 60 minutes. Now it's close to 20 percent of the game with players literally skating towards the bench or away from the bench and doing nothing else. There's no chance of scoring on almost 1 in 5 scoring chances when they are negated by players whose 30 seconds are up and they simply dump the puck in. They don't want to get caught on the ice. Okay, so why are they playing hockey? Teams are killing 20 percent of their own chances. Teams are willingly stopping an offensive chance and coaches are applauding it as a good play. It would be the equivalent of NBA players getting to half-court and just putting the ball down saying, "I need a breather, man. Please take the ball." It's absolutely bizarre. What is more bizarre is that no one has figured it out from the coaching side that these 30 second shifts are killing their offensive output. The best defense is a good offense which means if you keep the puck in the opponent's zone trying to score they won't be trying to score on you. It's a closed loop system with a limited space. There's only a finite amount of effort that can be exerted within the system. If you expel the inertia in immediacy then you must expect the automatic feedback which is the puck coming roaring back down the ice at you. If you took this to the extreme, hockey would turn into nothing but guys at centre ice shooting at a goalie once, have the puck rebound back to centre ice and letting the opponent shoot at your goalie and doing it every five seconds.

There is a finite amount of energy available per game per player. If a player can exert let's say 30 kilojoules of energy per one minute shift and there are 120 shifts of 30 seconds each in a 60 minute game then you have 720 kilojoules per game to spend. (Now that's not accurate because no one has measured the exact kilojoules exerted per game this is an example.) The point is it's finite. Almost a full 20 percent of a current NHL game, or 144 kilojoules is spent by each player simply skating with their backs to the play towards the bench. Goals are down about 20 percent from 2004.

There's only so many goals possible in a game of hockey given the size of the goalies and the size of the net, the size of the ice surface, how fast a player can skate and the time limit. It is measurable. And so what

I'm saying is if you dedicate so much finite energy to a conscious defensive effort then you're allocating a percentage of the outcome possibility. The more you close the loop on the defensive side the less is available on the offensive side. If your main concern is a constant whining about fresh legs on the ice then you remove offensive time.

There are variables, of course, given different talent levels. However, this is mitigated by several factors such as expansion, lack of talent in general, injuries and commonality. (Every team playing exactly the same way with minor variances.) There are also other factors such as having to pay offensive players more money in a salary cap era and so you may need to cap offense for financial reason. But I believe that is a minor factor albeit a real one.

A team burns 600 of its kilojoules per player on defense (skating to the bench considered defense.) Since they concede the puck some of that goes to the offense for the other team. Since the whole game is spent on the boards the defense isn't spent in their own zone. It starts way up ice with a dump in, then assuming defensive posture, skating backwards, chasing the puck, getting it to the redline and dumping it in and chasing. So it's actually making it harder for themselves. It's a feedback loop. They're causing a need for more defense. And so is the other team. And nothing ever gets done because 84% of the game is defense. The defense allows the other team to bring it out, then dump it in. Then their offense becomes defense. Around and around it goes.

And the best part of watching hockey, I think we can all agree, is the hockey itself. Hockey is the main attraction. People are buying tickets to watch hockey, or paying for cable channels or subscriptions to watch hockey. Players making moves. Tape to tape passes. Scoring chances at both ends. How many people pay to watch speed skating? It's not exactly a crowd pleaser and its tv audience is limited to winter Olympics when there's a national interest and people will watch almost anything. In the three years in between Olympics there's virtually no interest except for friends and family.

Players don't play hockey as much anymore as they do push the puck up ice. But where are they rushing too? There's only so much space on the ice as previously pointed out, they're rushing right through the scoring area to get to the boards to try to protect the puck with their backs mainly to the net and on their teammates. If the point is to score goals then it couldn't be done any worse. The confined space demands you play hockey chest forward and beat people one-on-one. You have to see what is going on to generate scoring opportunities. But NHL players spend the majority of their time with their backs to everyone else. It would be like a quarterback in the NFL turning around on the receivers and the offensive line and running away from the line of scrimmage then stopping briefly to throw a blind pass over his shoulder while not looking in the hopes it works out. The only reason why you would play the entire game with your back to everyone is to try to keep the puck as long as possible which again doesn't generate offensive opportunity. The whole purpose of being in the red zone is to score not to hack and whack it out on the boards. And if you break it down even further in a confined space the speed isn't making more than a half second difference. The reason players do this is because they can protect the puck against the boards and decrease the likelihood of a turnover.

The game is about angles and achieving the best possible angle to move the goalie and the defenseman so a shot on net can be achieved. You can't turn and burn going full speed to get this separation. All you really need to do is achieve the angle so that the puck can be shot or passed to a better scoring opportunity. NFL quarterback Peyton Manning was probably the best QB to ever play. He wasn't exactly fleet of foot and football is a very fast game. Yes it is different because he had an offensive line and there are no pick plays in hockey, although that has become a part of the game, with players struggling to create open ice and resorting to blocking for a teammate. Manning used his ability to play football rather than his prowess as an athlete. So does Tom Brady of the New England Patriots and before him was a guy playing in San Francisco named Joe Montana. They played the game chest forward. And hockey like football must be played knowing you will be hit. You have to see in front of you. I think some of the lost offense is due to players not wanting to get hit and lose the puck causing a turnover or simply just not wanting to get hit. When hockey loses its physicality and players wanting to get hit then it starts to die.

One of the lowest probability for scoring goals is to get across centre and shoot the puck in. Teammates must then determine if the puck is in a safe place and it's okay to proceed forward. The offensive players are so far behind the puck and the play that it is almost automatic that the other team is going to get the puck and bring it back out. It's extremely low percentage offensive hockey.

It is safe because there is no one supporting the puck in an offensive role. Logically, they are all in good defensive positions. But unfortunately if you're "all-in" on a defensive posture you can't be "all-in" on an offensive posture. So these players finally get the puck in the offensive zone and there's no commitment to offense so he can't do anything with the puck. At most, teams commit three players to offense while having all five back on defense. The fear is someone will turn the puck over trying to make a play and give up a breakaway going the other way which seems odd since all they've drafted are skaters so if anyone was capable of back checking to breakup the play it would surely be someone on the ice.

So a forward gets the puck deep in the offensive zone after dumping it in and then what? Who's he going to pass it to? No one else is likely to be with him. Most will have gone to the bench to change for fresh legs and defensemen are very unlikely to be in the slot in front of the net looking for a pass even though this is where Oilers defensemen great Paul Coffey and Boston Bruin great Bobby Orr made their livings. So the blueprint was made for these teams 50 years ago and they haven't followed the plans. The lessons of the past have been abandoned in the speed rush game.

When the centre-ice line was eliminated for the purposes of two-line passes in 2005, the defense had to retreat to guard against the stretch pass and keep in mind, the whole motto of today's NHL is defense. The thought process of removing the centre line was that it would cause more offense. But it did the opposite. There's very little support for the forwards on offense because the defenseman have retreated the moment they lose the puck in the offensive zone. The thought was that it would create more offense because people would make these long bomb passes without fear of a two-line pass but that's not what happened. Offense can't happen when you're too far ahead of the rest of the team and since the opposition is expecting you to do it then your blue liners are already hanging back to stay away from getting caught up ice. So now all you're doing is stretching the ice for a defensive posture. Yes you can make a 60 foot pass easier now but then it goes nowhere. Players are already back defending. And since they're back defending if the forward gets the puck he's all alone because his defenseman retreated already.

This "Trap busting" idea of shortening the neutral zone (by moving blue lines towards centre and removing the redline) backfired. All of the play happens in the neutral zone even more than it used to for example the Ottawa Senators in the 2017 playoffs played a full-on Trap and proved that removing the centre ice line made no difference to the Trap. The Senators continued on a 1-3-1 posture (one forward up guiding the opposition to either left or right) and with the three opponents in the neutral zone given a smaller surface to defend they were easily able to cut off the opponēnts. There was even less room for the offensive moving team to get through the neutral zone. Don't forget the offside at the blue line is still there so it creates a natural bottleneck at the blue line. The only way removing the red line and moving the blue line forward would actually work would be to cut all of the lines all together and dismiss offside. Then you really would have the ability to stretch pass. But the NHL didn't go that route and instead they stayed half-pregnant. And thank goodness because removing all the lines would turn hockey into a different sport.

Combined with the moving of the blue lines and the removal of the redlines was the touch-up or "tag up" offside rule created in 2005. What it means is that if you shoot the puck in the opponent's zone and there is one of their players in the zone then the play halts for the offensive player to get out of the zone so they can go back in and chase the puck "onside." Before this time the play was simply blown dead as a linesman would call the "hard" offside. Now the linesman puts his hand in the air and waits for the illegal player to get back onside, then they go back into the offensive zone. This has been a detriment to the league because it lends itself to dump and chase speed hockey.

Before 2005 coaches would be forced to let blue liners skate back into their own zone and start the offensive foray again because if you intentionally shot the puck in offside, knowing you had a player across the blue line before the puck, the faceoff would come all the way down the ice into your own zone. So blue liners had to have the ability to turn around and skate back into their own zone and try again, buying time for their teammates to get back onside of the blue line.

So now after 2005 what you can do is just dump the puck in and change up and then go and retrieve it or watch as the opponent just skates it back out of the zone.

Entire crops of defensemen have grown up now not
knowing how to drive an offense. They actually have
designated number one blue liners now whose specific
task is to carry the puck. All defenders used to have that
play in their back-pocket. Even the most rugged
defenders knew how to turn around, skate back through
the neutral zone, turn around again, and make a pass or
skate it back through the neutral zone, past the red line
and dump it in or skate it in. This rule change has
eliminated the offensive defenseman almost entirely
from the game. All they do is shoot the puck in. Nice and
simple.

The game demands the offense be driven from the
blue line because of the nature of the "house" blocking
in front of the net (where the defense puts all five guys
on the ice in front of their net) and so you can't get
anything done from down low. The only play that is
reliably open is the give and go - low, high, low - to a
blue liner. But since you're starting to really struggle to
get competent blue liners you're not seeing this happen.

As the game continues to gurgle around the toilet,
you're going to see desperate needs for blue liners. Since
they don't need to really defend anymore because the
forwards are now defensemen, I'm pretty surprised NHL
GMs and coaches are still drafting blue liners. What's the
point? Every single player they draft is "good
defensively" and lays down on the ice and blocks shots.
There isn't anything a defenseman can do that the
forward can't so why draft them? Eventually coaches are
going to figure out if you put five centres on the ice at
the same time you might spark an offense. Really, if I
were running a team I wouldn't draft anything but
centres and I would only put centres on the ice. And
once you head down that road of course the game ends
because how are you going to develop centres without
wingers and defensemen when they know they aren't
going to get drafted to the NHL?

Coaches have ventured into this pool a little bit by icing four forwards on a power play. But I think it's only a matter of time where they figure it out that there are no blue liners worth drafting or playing in their systems and so therefore you might as well drop them. That's where the game is now where this conversation about dropping blue liners altogether isn't stupid. It's just in the infancy of developing as everyone realizes there is no need for hitting in the game now and anyone can just dump a puck in. You might as well put a "good hands" team on the ice hoping for some kind of offense.

The blue lines and centre ice line are really where the offensive hockey players make their money because this is where mistakes are made. They are turnover zones. It forces actions because of the offsides. A defender must make a decision to either stop the intrusion or backup. These decisions are where the good offensive hockey players will strike. They usually have a very good change of pace in speed. Their ability to shift speeds at the blue line can freeze a defender and create separation and not necessarily by going faster. By removing the centre line as a place of opportunity they have created less room in the enclosed system. If you think of these areas on the ice as a danger zone on a battlefield, a place which must be defended because of the opportunity to flank on either side and proceed unhindered to the home castle, there is only one danger zone left in front of the castle. And so if the defender also knows they will give up the blue line and entrench in front of the net in the danger zone, you really don't have any offensive zones anywhere. These rule changes collapsed the offense like a cheap tent.

Offsides are a two-way street. The defender uses this as a tool to defend but the offensive player uses that against them as an opportunity. They eliminated it with this "out" of dumping it in and playing it safe. Hockey isn't meant to be a "safe" game. If it were, then fighting wouldn't be a part of the game and there wouldn't be boards. The rule changes meant to help the offense worked against it with full Traps and less available opportunity for the snipers and more importantly fewer players growing their offensive games. They helped bad defenseman stay in the game because anyone can wrist a puck in deep. They don't have to turn and get caught by a skilled player. They're not forced into decisions. It's such a simple game now.

OVERTIME SHOOTOUTS

Overtime and shootouts in the NHL regular season instead of win, loss and tie dries up offense. In 1999 they moved to Wins, Loss, Ties, OT (a point awarded for making it to OT.) (In 2005 they went to three columns - W L OT). The bonus point was given for winning in OT and added to the normal Win column. They tried to produce a winner every game but they added two winners every night, usually, because of the loser point. And so teams scramble for those loser points by killing the game defensively to get it to OT. You can not lose an NHL game in 60 minutes and survive. Teams MUST get the loser points to make the playoffs.

And it warps the league standings. In January of 2017, 26 of the 30 NHL teams were above .500. That should be impossible except for the loser point. The result is that some games are worth three points and some are worth two points. And it is a significant problem because what was lost is the ability for fans to determine what is a good team and a bad team. Perhaps more importantly good teams could identify bad teams. And the most important thing coaches and teams know today is if you're going to lose don't lose in regulation time. Get that single point every game! Get it to overtime at a minimum. And so it stresses defense of course.

When there are really bad teams in the NHL, chaos is created from GM firings to coach firings to massive player changes. In other words it forced change and it forced teams to make these changes on the fly to save face. There were massive trades of players during the season as teams did everything they could to spark a winning streak. You had real highs and real lows in the game.

The loser point has evened this out to a nice steady mediocrity. Anyone can look at the standings almost to the last week of the season and see that they are "still in the hunt" for a playoff spot. When in reality they are not. But it appears as if it's possible. So teams that would play all their kids and give up a ton of goals don't do it anymore. In the 1980s, teams could score 400 goals per season but there were many teams that could give up nearly 400 goals per season. And that's exciting. It means 10-1 blowouts. Nowadays every game is a 2-1 game or a series of mistakes to get it to 3-2. What would you rather watch? A 10-1 blowout or a 2-1 snooze fest? The blowout is spectacular viewing. Tempers flare on the ice and fights can break out. Coaches lose their minds on the bench, goaltenders are pulled, put back in, pulled again. It's terrifically entertaining. Almost every visiting team is bringing a 50 goal scorer and a 100 point player. There were stars in the game. But not anymore with every game being a "playoff" game. The regular season is dead as we knew it.

It's a terrible mistake to think that by keeping the standings close fans will be sucked in to watch a bad team because they are still "in it" right to the bitter end. Really good hockey fans such as in Vancouver or Ottawa don't appear to be buying it. The Ottawa Senators went to the Conference Finals and were having trouble selling tickets. They were terrible to watch. Other teams such as New York, Dallas or Los Angeles are event cities where fans expect hockey stars not necessarily winning hockey. Big cities require big entertainment. And whether it's losing or winning, they pay to see entertainment value on the ice. They want to see the big scorers come in and put up a few goals. You can be a fan of a certain team and go to the game knowing they're going to lose but knowing it's going to be really good entertainment value. I don't believe anybody willingly pays hockey to see a 1-0 game with 15 shots each. It's not a goaltender battle. It's just a big ... ughhhh on the ice.

The best way to achieve some level of entertainment is by having a winner and a loser every night. If you don't create this I don't think you develop real hockey fans in your home market. You need the agony of going through four or five 50 point seasons to appreciate the 110 point seasons. A 100 point team should be a real juggernaut and before the overtimes and shootouts they were real powerhouses. It's not so anymore. There are no really good teams because the winners and losers are pushed together. Everyone gets a point, enjoy yourselves. It's why President Trophy winners rarely win the Stanley Cup.

It also takes offense out of the game because one of the cards losing teams could play is having a couple of 100 point players or kids scoring 40 or 50 goals. But with every team in the playoff race right to the bitter end you don't have any impetus to play the kids and try to score goals for entertainment's sake. It's the damn the torpedoes full speed ahead mentality that creates excitement. You need these teams with great young kids getting pasted every night but providing supreme entertainment value for home and away crowds alike.

Every single night you have the same thing in every single arena, almost. You know what's going to happen. The first team that scores wins, usually, and gets up to a two or three goal lead, then gets hit by penalties, and the other team scores late and pulls their goalie and falls a goal short or ties it up and loses in overtime or shootout.

Blah. It's the same thing every night with the same colours in almost every arena too because the home team always wears their away colours. Blah, blah, blah. One player will get 50 goals, usually Alexander Ovechkin, and one player might scrape to 100 points. Blah, blah, blah. And every team will be ever so close to getting into the playoffs. It's boring. There is a redeeming value to seeing a really bad team come to town because the home team might score goals. They might be playing a wide open style of game as they play a bunch of kids. The anticipation of a blowout is a good thing. Diversity is a good thing in hockey.

Some people may say, well, if you go down that road to the NBA of just Wins and Losses you could end up in dire straits. Yes, true, if you take it far enough you do have a situation where an entire league is uncompetitive. But I would argue a lot of other things went into the NBA to make it so bad, some of which is cultural. And by that I mean I'm not sure there is a competitive spirit in basketball, for example, resting star players during the regular season. I think you'd have a hard time pulling a star player out of a hockey game, although it does happen for "injuries" that happen at convenient times such as All-Star games. The other thing is the NBA isn't really a team game. Yes, you need to put five guys on the court, but it's really only required to have one or two superstars. And the NBA salary cap allows for "stacked" teams. The NHL salary cap does not.

In the WLT time a single point for a tie was a very impressive thing for teams in the bottom half of the league. It meant something. You could leave a game after a good tie and feel very good about the outcome. Now you're almost guaranteed of a circus time outcome, well, it just seems like that. The actual statistic is about 24% of the time the NHL goes to overtime. And if you consider only New Jersey Devils were below .500 when scoring the first goal, in 2017 that's pretty bad. What it tells you is that if you score the first goal you're almost guaranteed a single point. So what happens? Teams spiral into a death wobble trying to score the first goal and then to defend the first goal because it matters so much. The NHL tried to please Americans not used to ties in football, baseball or basketball. But I think they also tried to keep the tie to please Canadians. It ended up just being a mess.

Teams may skate from end-to-end faster than they have before giving the appearance that they are doing something but they're really not. It's all for show for people who don't know much about hockey quite frankly. Hockey is meant to be played in the middle of the ice, not on the boards. The closer to the boards the safer the play and that's where the coaches want it. And if you dig guys just skating back and forth then, hey, you like the game.

But if you like the actual game of hockey, then you want more. You want it all to end in 60 minutes - winner takes all or split. The other sports end it in 60. Extra time in the NFL is extremely rare. The NBA doesn't take players off the court for OT or have shootouts. Soccer is 90 minutes (and would you want a minute more?). I'll admit World Cup soccer in overtime is good entertainment. But it's not fun to watch below the level of the World Cup. And then there's the ugly shootout afterwards.

And for some reason hockey took the dreaded shootout from soccer and put it in its game. The concept was to provide entertainment and a winner but does anyone appreciate it now? Teams can get 12 shooters in and you're thinking, please, God, anyone, just score a goal. The longer it goes the more it proves how inept these NHL players are. It's there for everyone to see that the forwards are clueless on breakaways and the goalies are way better than they are at hockey.

It makes the games excruciatingly long. It's getting into dangerous cricket times. And of course, someone has to play the game on the ice whether it's four on four or three on three. (The first five minutes of OT are four on four, the second five minutes is three on three. And that in itself is ridiculous because it's not hockey). The extra time played may not be a problem for the Toronto Maple Leafs because they rarely travel but if you're a west coast hockey team like the San Jose Sharks it's going to make one hell of a difference to your season. The time adds up. And if you have an older team it's going to get worse.

And now the overtimes have been coached to a halt. Teams actually learned to play man on man in the OT to get it to SO just because they're in survival mode. And so OT bogged right down to first gear when it was supposed to be high-speed entertainment. Then they went to farcical three-on-three hockey. You never see three-on-three in the regular season during regulation time; it was theoretical. But then to bring it out as a way to decide an extra point? Wouldn't it be better to just go Win, Loss, Tie after 60 minutes?

Since these extra points are handed out willy nilly because some games are worth three points and some are worth two points (a 2-1 OTL means three points were handed out and a 2-0 loss means only two points were handed out) then you really can't look at the standings. You would think winning the regular season and getting a President's Trophy would be an indication of playoff success. But the exact opposite is true. In the last 17 seasons only four President Trophy winners have won a Stanley Cup and that includes two by Detroit with Nicklas Lidstrom and the remnants of a high salary verses everyone else. The other was Colorado with Peter Forsberg and a high salary team pre-2005 salary cap era. Only the Chicago Blackhawks and Detroit Red Wings have done it post salary cap era with arguably the two best defenseman to play the game in Lidstrom and Chicago's Duncan Keith. So you have to have historically good offensive defenseman to pull off the feat of winning both the regular season and playoff season. In the NFL you can expect the really good teams to win the Super Bowl with the odd exception but it is the exception not the rule. You know who the good teams are in the NFL. The NBA is an extreme where you know who will win the championship before the season even starts because free agents are allowed to stack teams because of their lax free agency rules. But the NHL is random.

Overtime started in the NHL in 1983 with the loser getting no points until the 1999/2000 season where the loser got a point until the shootout was introduced in 2005/2006 season where both teams still got a minimum of one point. And so the ability to read how teams were doing ended in 1983. You could actually look at the win total of a team and know they had actually won that many games and lost that many games in 60 minutes. Starting in 1999 it started to get hazy because was a win in 60 minutes or 65 minutes? A fan would have a hard time knowing.

Then after the 2006 season the NHL history book was tossed into the garbage can because of the two or three point games. Teams got an overtime loss stat which wasn't the same as a loss in regulation time. The NHL added a fourth column in 1999. MLB and NBA have two columns, wins and losses, while the NFL also has two columns, however they do have the ability to tie but on average there are two ties per regular season for the entire 32 team league, so it's pretty much wins and losses. And then there's the NHL with four columns which they changed to three columns in 2005. If you followed all that then hurrah.

These rule changes have only hurt offense, and made it hard to follow and in the American sports media eyes it must make it appear silly. And it is silly. It's a system of artificially keeping teams close in the standings to create the illusion that there is parity when in reality it's not parity. If it were parity then Los Angeles, Pittsburgh, and Chicago wouldn't have won the Stanley Cup seven of the last eight years. Chicago and Los Angeles having the two best defensemen in the game and Pittsburgh having Evgeni Malkin and speedy plumbers. There's only the illusion of parity.

EXPANSION

It would be fairly easy to just pose the question: Why? and end this chapter. Why though? The NHL is trying to move to 32 teams and the last expansion team, Las Vegas, apparently paid $550 million US for an expansion team to become number 31. And so there's the why because it's not the product on the ice that's benefitting. This is exactly backwards for an entertainment model, at least for hockey lovers. Why though? There isn't enough talent coming from the feeder systems to provide for entertainment. But it is understandable. It's a lot of money and the NHL is a free enterprise business and so they're free to do as they wish. But who's standing up for the fans?

I suppose there is the argument it makes the league look bigger by having as many teams as the NFL and more than the NBA or MLB. And there is the argument that if you can sell an expansion team for half a billion dollars then it makes existing teams worth more than an expansion team, in theory, so I think we can all understand the rationale for trying to expand the NHL.

And the NHL can use the threat of expansion to leverage new NHL buildings. If you don't replace our aging building we may have to move this franchise. The Calgary Flames right now are trying to get a new taxpayer funded building and they ratcheted up the pressure on Calgary the same day a new Seattle redevelopment of Key Arena for possible NHL team was announced. Other leagues do this to it is not unique to the NHL. And to be honest, it's a fairly good business practice if you discount how much it upsets fans in the city potentially losing their team.

But without the entertainment value to go along with expansion many of these franchises fall flat on their faces, an example being Arizona which had to be propped up by the NHL for years. This example is not unique to the NHL, with the NBA and MLB also having their difficulties over the years. But NBA teams are worth over $1 billion and most MLB teams are also worth $1 billion. The NHL lags far behind in value. Could you buy an NHL team for less than the $500 million Las Vegas allegedly paid? If you believe reports about the Carolina Hurricanes then yes, quite possibly. Forbes Magazine reporter Mike Ozanian wrote on Nov. 13, 2014, that "...a year ago Vincent Viola acquired another troubled NHL team, the Florida Panthers, for an enterprise value (equity plus net debt) of just $160 million..." Ozanian also reports that the Arizona Coyotes sold for $304 million but the price has not been officially confirmed. So that's a far cry from the $1 billion price tag of an NBA team and the reported cost of an NHL expansion team.

I would argue the best way to increase the NHL teams values is to stock them with talent and have highly entertaining games. It requires being able to ice 20 players of exceptional quality. And so if you increase the players in the NHL from 690 to 713 (23 man roster) then you're obviously going to be watering the product down. Coaches scramble on defense to scrape together wins because winning keeps jobs when the product pool is lacking. Coaches and GMs are forced to do more with less and the product on the ice doesn't get better as we've seen from previous expansions. Scoring was at its peak in the NHL with 21 teams. As the league expanded to 30 we've seen scoring steadily decrease. It just makes sense because in order to move the puck from tape-to-tape with high speed and efficiency you need a high degree of talent on the ice on the same team at the same time. The more you spread the talent out the worse it gets.

You can't develop kids anymore. The expansion trickled down to the American Hockey League, the NHL feeder system, as well because they are losing talent to the new NHL club and its new AHL affiliate. In order to develop kids you have to play offensive hockey, which means a level of talent and coaches committed to developing not winning. And since winning, not developing, is how you get promoted to the NHL it's just a waste of time to send kids to the AHL. They don't have talent to play with or coaches who want to run and gun.

Combine the AHL slide with the beginning of the Kontinental Hockey League in Russia and Swedish Elite League and you're really in a talent crunch. If the KHL expansion into China grows rapidly it's going to be really thin gruel. The problem at the AHL level is exasperated because you're trying to teach kids how to score, or they should be learning to score.

If you're a winger in the AHL, and just for arguments sake I'll pick a Canuck prospect, a 5th overall draft pick, Jake Virtanen, who was sent to the AHL and really struggled. I would argue he struggled because the Canucks' farm team in Utica had almost no centres for him to play with, and certainly no talent to speak of from an NHL point of view. Darren Archibald led Utica Comets, where Virtanen played, with 23 goals and 47 points in the 2016/17 season. No disrespect to Archibald, but that's pretty low for an entire season in a development league. And so how's Virtanen going to develop down in Utica? What's he going to learn? I would suggest he's going to learn sweet F all down on a team without any talent, again no disrespect meant. I'm sure they're all really hardworking guys and Virtanen can learn what it's like to toil in the minors. But is it really a benefit?

So you have a double whammy going on. Players are dumped into the NHL before they're ready right out of junior because they're cheap cannon fodder and players sent to the AHL may get marginally better but that's about it. The last great player to come out of the AHL after spending two years there was? Exactly, not many.

I think it's fair to say goalies still develop in the AHL. But if you think about it why wouldn't they? They aren't seeing much better talent in the NHL. They get maybe 24 shots per night, eight shots per period, one shot every two or three minutes. It's pretty rare teams give up more than 30 shots in a game. And because the players are better trained in the NHL into their defensive handcuffs you rarely see better chances than the AHL. Goalies come up and have immediate impacts, for example the Pittsburgh Penguins goalie Matt Murray has played 62 regular season games but has two Stanley Cups after three full years in the AHL.

But when is the last time a forward was called up from the AHL and popped 50 goals in the NHL? It's been a long time since someone came up and was an immediate impact "carry a team" type of hockey player. Some people may say the Leafs Mitch Marner and Willem Nylander but without Auston Matthews they're still toiling in the minors, aren't they? And neither player crested 25 goals. And it comes down to goals. Did you pop 40 or 50 goals? Not even close and at times they looked like they should be back in the AHL.

Bernie Nicholls is the perfect example of a player who went to the AHL, scored 41 goals in 55 games in New Haven of the AHL, came back the next year for Los Angeles and scored 28 goals and when Gretzky arrived he pumped 70. Bernie pumped 152 points in juniors in his draft year of 1981. When you compare Nicholls to Marner it's pretty laughable.

Thirteen NHL players scored over 100 points in 1985; there was one in 2016/17, one in 2015/16 and none in 2014/15. There were 19 players in the 1985 season with 90 points or more and 30 players were at a point per game or better. Of course 1985 was the year Gretzky popped 215 points a mere 74 points ahead of the next guy. It's a significant fall to where the NHL is at now.

The NHL had a good track record of 100 years of producing goal scorers. And now you don't. Quite possibly the greatest player to ever play the game, Nels Stewart, came from the Cleveland USAHA affiliate to the Montreal Maroons of the NHL in 1925/26 at the age of 23 and scored 34 goals in 36 games and added 119 pims. Stewart held the NHL goal scoring record for 25 years when he left the NHL in 1940 scoring 324 goals in 652 games. (Incidentally, why the NHL doesn't celebrate every NHL player's 324th goal by stopping the game and awarding a Nels Stewart Trophy to him is beyond me.)

Expansion causes fan fatigue as key matchups of marquee teams happen less frequently. With the loser point being awarded and the teams bunched up fighting for playoff spots all the teams become the same. There's less likely to be a really good top line on a visiting team and so home crowds can start to fatigue at the ticket gate and tv ratings can drop; in the 1993/94 season ABC had a 1.7 TV Ratings Share for the NHL and by 2004 it was down to 1.1 rating (either one is pretty abysmal.) There's hockey everywhere and it's all the same product. There really are no mismatches as the games water down and defense rules. There is usually only 15 points separating top to bottom in the standings. Upsets aren't really upsets anymore. Neither team playing has a 100 point player or 50 goal scorer. It's just a bunch of guys playing a bunch of guys. And then what are you building towards during the season? President Trophy teams don't win Stanley Cups (often) so what's the point?

It's also a point of anger for fans knowing these expansion teams are getting draft picks needed for their own team and knowing there isn't enough talent to go around from the feeder leagues already. The more you add the expansion teams the more likely it is your team is going to be bad and stay bad because the draft is not going to help. And it's more competition for scarce free agents.

Fans may also have players scooped from their favourite team in the expansion draft. As a fan in St. Louis, Vancouver or Buffalo, you could be close to 50 years of supporting your team without winning only to see these new teams scoop up the available talent and win Stanley Cups. Smart hockey fans know there is a cycle of winning and losing and if you're on a down cycle which doesn't correspond to a franchise player then you'll never win. It's why Edmonton and Pittsburgh keep winning Stanley Cups or look to be headed that way in the case of Edmonton. They are on extreme cycles of losing/bankruptcy which reward with Stanley Cups because they are in the losing when the franchise player comes to the draft and there's no expansion.

If the team never crashes to the bottom and stays there for 10 years it will likely never win a Stanley Cup if the NHL has expanded. Recent Cup winners Pittsburgh and Los Angeles faced dire ownership issues. The more expansion teams you add then the longer you have to bottom out before you get a franchise hockey player which comes down the pipe every 10 years if you're lucky. And it puts the franchise in peril. The NFL can support 32 teams because their first round draft provides an impact football player but more importantly they're still getting impact players in their 5th and 6th rounds of drafting. The percentage chance of a player taken in the NHL's 5th round of making the NHL for one game, let alone being a star, is less than 10 percent. The more teams you add the more the percentage drops because the player pool isn't expanding in the feeder leagues.

As I've stated you've got a competing KHL in Russia taking a lot of its own Russian players and is potentially expanding into China. The Czechslovakia hockey program split up when the countries split up, and the Swedish program hasn't advanced size wise. The American program is growing but it's still in its infancy. There's really only a few states with NCAA hockey.

The other weird thing about expansion in the NHL is every expansion draft is different. There's no rhyme or reason for how they decide to divvy up the current crop of players. Teams in their down cycles will be kicked to the curb more than the ones already out of the draft and entering the playoffs when the NHL expands. For example, the Las Vegas expansion draft really impacted the Vancouver Canucks, who were the 29th placed team. The Toronto Maple Leafs and Edmonton Oilers were not impacted because they're out of the draft players mode. They got Matthews and McDavid.

Arizona was smacked in the face by expansion. They were dropped in the lottery draft by Las Vegas. If Vegas had been approved two years earlier it would have impacted the Boston Bruins and if it was one year earlier it would have impacted the Toronto Maple Leafs. But expansion was done while Vancouver and Arizona and a few other teams were trying to rebuild through the draft.

And yet these bottom place teams were treated the same as those teams in the top 10, as if they had players to lose in the expansion draft. For example the Vancouver Canucks lost Luca Sbisa, a good solid defenseman and the only rugged blue liner they had who wasn't injured. It was a significant loss for them because they're a terrible team at the time of the draft and couldn't afford to lose anyone, at all. And because they're on the bottom of their cycle, they couldn't offer a first round draft pick to save a player because they're picking in the top 5 in 2017 and 2018, likely.

The Chicago Blackhawks traded a first round pick to protect a young player from being taken in the expansion draft. Their pick was so late in the draft it's already a longshot. But a bad team like Vancouver's first round pick would have meant a Top 5 pick to protect Sbisa, which they obviously couldn't do, and so they lost more than Chicago. It's virtually no fee at all to keep their prized young talent in Chicago. On the other hand Sbisa might anchor the Vegas blue line for a decade. Sbisa was what the Canucks got in trade return for their star centre Ryan Kesler, and so now they have no one on their roster to show for trading Kesler (I realize they also got Nick Bonino in the Kesler trade who they traded for Brandon Sutter who hasn't performed well.)

So expansion cycles have affected teams differently. The Nashville expansion year occurred in 1998 when, again, a Vancouver Canucks team was rebuilding along with the New York Islanders and Washington Capitals. The 1991 expansion draft of the San Jose Sharks and 1993 North Stars move to Dallas affected the Buffalo Sabres, Hartford Whalers and Quebec Nordiques who were trying to rebuild. Hartford moved to Carolina in 1997 and Quebec moved to Colorado in 1995. Buffalo has tenaciously battled to keep its team in Buffalo. Again in 1992/93 when the Ottawa Senators and Anaheim Mighty Ducks joined the league, Buffalo was again hit along with the Hartford Whalers. The Nordiques moved to fourth spot in the draft but didn't win a Stanley Cup and moved. You could make the argument it impacted Quebec, Buffalo and Hartford the hardest. Interestingly the team least impacted by all expansion drafts appears to be the Pittsburgh Penguins, and perhaps correspondingly, have five Stanley Cups to the Buffalo Sabres and Washington Capitals none.

It's the teams in the bottom 10 of the standings who have been there for two years or more who get kicked by expansion. The Buffalo Sabres have probably been impacted more than any other team with the St. Louis

Blues second and Vancouver Canucks third. Teams needing the draft suddenly find another 10 teams beside them. And the expansion cycle has corresponded to the down cycles of these three teams specifically.

Each team gets a share of the expansion fee money. But some teams pay way more than the other teams. A team like Pittsburgh or Toronto or Edmonton will pocket the expansion money no problem. But a team like Vancouver or Buffalo is going to be hit hard at the ticket gates probably for more than the expansion fee would pay them. For some teams expansion is going to be a financial loss and there doesn't seem to be an equitable attempt by the NHL at making it financially right for these teams. In other words, those rebuilding teams should get more expansion fee money than the ones not rebuilding yet.

Expansion teams often dumb the game down at their arenas. They bring in mascots and cheerleaders and try to get people to come in for anything but the hockey. (I'm not against entertainment in the building, I'm arguing for it, but cheerleaders? It's kind of sexist.) You hear announcements on the public address system saying, "Your team is on the power play!" Uggh, really? It's embarrassing and makes the NHL seem third rate; does the NFL pa announcer scream - your Kansas City Chiefs are on the field goal team! And when an expansion team's novelty wears off the crowds can become thin and if your favourite team is visiting their arena you're looking around at a depressing scene. And then comes the inevitable, "we can't make money" announcement and the team is put up for sale which again humiliates the league and damages the product in places where people really love hockey because they're all a part of the NHL.

Expansion has had success though. Nashville and San Jose are two cities that have really embraced the NHL but they have yet to go through an extended period of missing the playoffs so then we'll see what happens.

Columbus is a very good hockey market but then again, it's had hockey for decades and decades, so it's not surprising.

If you think of the NHL as a sole business where they are all together then why don't they have yearly expansion drafts for teams getting into the 50 years without a Stanley Cup bracket? There's just no teamwork in the league to even things up in Washington, St. Louis, Buffalo and Vancouver. You would think at some point someone would say, "you know... they've been in the league for a long time here after expansion... people are dying off never seeing a Stanley Cup in their city..." You would think these are progressive business people and would realize, hey, we might be there at some time too, let's have the "it's been a long time since we won anything" expansion draft. It's not really a team of franchises working together. Once a team gets to 30 years of futility, the league should step in and start taking action such as awarding extra first round draft picks. There is such a scarce amount of talent in the NHL it would be difficult to convince the other owners in Pittsburgh, Chicago and New York it is in their best interest to make sure teams don't get to 100 years without a championship. The Vancouver Canucks are over 100 years without a Stanley Cup and 50 years without a Lester Patrick Cup (WHL professional league - rival of the NHL league). The NFL, MLB and NBA don't do it either, which is also pretty stupid. The NFL should be taking care of Buffalo. Poor Buffalo. Unlike the NHL the NFL does have the draft depth to do it.

Adam Silver, NBA commissioner, talking about expansion in a CBS article with Matt Moore talks about each team having a requirement for all 30 teams in the NBA being "must-see" experiences. What are the "must-see" experiences in the NHL? Silver is very worried about the fan experience for the NBA. Where's the concern for fan experience in the NHL?

Cities clamour for an expansion team believing it will help their economy but the new sports franchise may not help cities financially. This is from a report called "What Are the Benefits of Hosting a Major League Sports Franchise?" By Jordan Rappaport and Chad Wilkerson, 2001.

"In response to the shortcomings of such impact studies, independent economists have attempted to measure the effect of professional sports teams on metro areas in a number of ways. One method is to compare growth rates of metro areas with and without professional teams, after controlling for other variables. For example, in a study of the growth of per capita personal income in 48 metro areas from 1958 to 1987, Baade (1994) found no significant difference between metro areas with major league teams and those without. In a study of 46 metro areas from 1990 to 1994, Walden actually found a negative relationship between economic activity and the presence of a sports team.

A second way of measuring the impact of teams is to examine the subsequent growth of cities that acquire new teams. Baade and Sanderson did this for ten metro areas that obtained new franchises between 1958 and 1993 and found no significant increases in employment or output. Results from Coates and Humphreys showed that per capita income fell when metro areas added teams."

Should any professional sports team have a duty to positively impact its surrounding and supporting city? Probably not. It's a free market system and everyone is entitled to open their own business and fail or succeed based on their own merits and hard work. But it does make you think about the impact an NHL team would have in a city like San Jose for example. Is it taking money from the economy or generating money for the economy? If people are spending ticket money and entertainment money in San Jose at an NHL game what are they not spending the money on? It is a closed system. People have a finite amount of disposable income. In Toronto, for example, you could argue the Toronto Blue Jays from MLB killed the Toronto Argonauts of the Canadian Football League. It may have had a trickle down effect into the Vancouver market as the Vancouver market appears to also be rejecting the CFL possibly because Toronto deems the CFL as a minor league sport. And it's also happening in Montreal.

And while there are benefits to the minor leagues of hockey because another AHL affiliate may be born (they may also share an affiliate and not outright own one) in terms of jobs for hockey players it should be pointed out the product in the AHL also suffers for their fans.

So I can see the argument on both sides of the coin with people believing more teams in the US helps expose the product to new fans so you should expand. The other side of the coin is you have to keep those fans. If they go in, see one game, and it sucks then what is the impact on them returning? Or loving the game? There is a finite number of potential customers. Goals sell hockey. Fighting sells hockey. Hitting sells hockey. Especially in the minors. It's hard to do when you start spreading the talent so thin. There is a breaking point where existing markets begin to suffer talent fatigue and I worry the NHL has found it.

RULE CHANGES

The NHL allows the GMs of the teams to get together every year and make rule changes. It isn't done this way in MLB, NBA or NFL. Why would it be done by GMs? They're often fired and they have their own agendas. A GM of a large defensive team is going to have an agenda which favours a large defensive team. If you have a really good goalie you'll want a game that favours goalies. And so presumably what happens at the GM meetings is each GM pushing and pulling the rules in their favour.

Not all GMs are created equal. Some have more power than others and more influence than others. For example, Boston Bruins owner Jeremy Jacobs has owned the team since 1975 and is the current Chairman, NHL board of governors. Jacobs was recently influential in a proposed revamping of the Key Arena in Seattle as a pre-amble to an NHL team in Seattle, moving him ahead of others who had offered new arenas for Seattle with private money for years. That's pretty influential. It's also said Jacobs can be very vocal and demonstrative with the other owners, especially new ones. Jacobs was against the NHL going to the Olympics in South Korea and in 2017 NHL commissioner Gary Bettman announced they would not be going to South Korea.

Jacobs is known as a hard liner on labour discussions and the NHL has had multiple labour disruptions. The NHL commissioner was first elected in 1993 (there was no commissioner prior to this year) and he answers to the Board of Governors headed by Jacobs. Given the owner of the Bruins is a powerful and ranking figure in the NHL the GM of the Bruins is likely going to have more influence than other GMs.

And so you have this group of GMs all getting together to discuss rule changes but each one owning a bias to their team, naturally, and with some having more influence than others. Although I'm sure these GMs try not to be biased and do what is best for the game and also try to be fair it is human nature to protect your turf because it's their job. And the other point is: If you always meet, twice per year, to discuss rule changes you're likely going to make rule changes, otherwise, why are you meeting? The NFL selects eight people from the coaching, management and ownership ranks to oversee competition and suggest rule changes to the commissioner. They take input from college ranks, experts, medical fields, data from injury lists, trainers, and the NFL Players Association. It's really detailed and comprehensive. And I think by excluding most teams directly there's a sense of obligation to the other members when they are selected to the committee. No system is perfect. But I think the NFL has it closer to being right because some of the members are at the top level with a view of growing the pot of money for the NFL which grows the value of their franchise. They've also been revenue sharing a lot longer than the NHL. Being an owner of an NFL team means thinking of the NFL as an overall entity and not a group of individual members. I'm not sure the NHL is there yet.

The NHL GMs have been pretty busy. These are just some of the rule changes in the past 10 years alone that I could gather, some of it from the NHL's web page written by NHL writer Dan Rosen of NHL.com:

2005-06

(1)   The center line was eliminated for two-line passes, and the tag up offside rule was reinstated.

(2)   Restrictions on the goaltender playing the puck outside a designated area were introduced.

(3)   The team icing the puck was disallowed from substituting for the next faceoff.

(4)   A shootout was introduced if the game remained tied after the five-minute overtime.

(5)   Goaltender's equipment was downsized.

2016 3-on-3 Overtime

1. Teams play an additional overtime period of not more than five (5) minutes with the team scoring first declared the winner and being awarded an additional point.

2. The overtime period will be played with each team at 3-on-3 manpower (plus goaltender) for the full five-minute period.

3. Manpowers during overtime will be adjusted to reflect the situation in the game, but at no time will a team have fewer than three (3) skaters on the ice during the overtime period. For example, if a team enters the overtime period on a power play, manpower would be adjusted from 5 on 4 at the end of regulation to 4 on 3 at the start of overtime. If a minor penalty is assessed during overtime, the teams will play 4 on 3. If a second minor penalty is assessed to the same team during overtime, the teams will play 5 on 3.

4. If the game remains tied at the end of the five (5) minute overtime period, the teams will proceed to a three-round shootout. After each team has taken three shots, if the score remains tied, the shootout will proceed to a "sudden death" format.

5. Clubs who pull their goaltender for an extra attacker during the overtime period (other than on a delayed penalty) will be subject to the potential

forfeiture of their one (1) point earned for the tie at the end of regulation in the event the opposing team scores into the empty net.

6. At the end of regulation, the entire ice surface will be shoveled and the goalies will change ends. There will be no further ice surface maintenance during the balance of overtime period. Following the overtime period and before the shootout, the ice surface will be shoveled again, and the goalies will change ends.

Expanded Video Review

This expanded video review is intended to be extremely narrow in scope and the original call on the ice is to be overturned if, and only if, a determination is made by the on-ice Official(s) (in consultation with the Toronto Video Room) that the original call on the ice was not correct. If a review is not conclusive and/or there is any doubt whatsoever as to whether the call on the ice was correct, the on-ice Official(s) will be instructed to confirm their original call.

Coach's Challenge

1. A team may only request a Coach's Challenge to review the following scenarios:

a) "Off-Side" Play Leading to a Goal. A play that results in a "GOAL" call on the ice where the defending team asserts that the play should have been stopped by reason of an "Off-Side" infraction by the attacking team.

b) Scoring Plays Involving Potential "Interference on the Goalkeeper"

(i) A play that results in a "GOAL" call on the ice where the defending team asserts that the goal should have been disallowed due to "Interference on the Goalkeeper," as described in Rules 69.1, 69.3 and 69.4; or

(ii) A play that results in a "NO GOAL" call on the ice despite the puck having entered the net, where the on-ice Officials have determined that the attacking team was guilty of "Interference on the Goalkeeper" but where the attacking team asserts: (i) there was no actual contact of any kind initiated by an attacking Player with the goalkeeper; or (ii) the attacking Player was pushed, shoved, or fouled by a defending Player causing the attacking Player to come into contact with the goalkeeper; or (iii) the attacking Player's positioning within the goal crease did not impair the goalkeeper's ability to defend his goal and, in fact, had no discernible impact on the play.

2. A team may only request a Coach's Challenge if they have their time-out available and the Coach's Challenge must be effectively initiated prior to the resumption of play.

3. If the Coach's Challenge does not result in the original call on the ice being overturned, the team exercising such challenge will forfeit its time-out.

4. If the Coach's Challenge does result in the call on the ice being overturned, the team successfully exercising such challenge will retain its time-out.

League Initiated Review

1. In the final minute of play in the 3rd Period and at any point in Overtime (Regular Season and Playoffs), Hockey Operations will initiate the review of any scenario that would otherwise be subject to a Coach's Challenge.

2. Hockey Operations will continue to initiate and be responsible for the review of all goals subject to Video Review under Rule 38.4. Where a Coach's Challenge is available on a scoring play potentially involving "Interference on the Goalkeeper" or "Off-Side," Hockey Operations will, as an initial and threshold matter, determine that the puck entered the net and is a good hockey goal before the play will be subject to further review by means of a Coach's Challenge (or, in the final minute of play or in Overtime, a review initiated by Hockey Operations). If a team requests a Coach's

Challenge but Video Review under Rule 38.4 renders such Challenge unnecessary, then the Challenge will be deemed not to have been made and the timeout will be preserved.

2014 rule changes

Rule 1.8 – Rink - Goalkeeper's Restricted Area

The trapezoid will be expanded by two feet from the goal post on both sides of the net.

Rule 1.9 – Rink – Face-off Spots and Circles – Ice Markings/Hash Marks

The hash marks at the end zone circles will be moved from three feet apart to five feet, seven inches apart (international markings).

Rule 23 – Game Misconduct Penalties

A new Game Misconduct category will be created. Clipping, charging, elbowing, interference, kneeing, head-butting and butt-ending move from the general category into the same category as boarding and checking from behind ("Physical Fouls"), whereby a player who incurs two such game misconducts in this category would now be automatically suspended for one game.

Rule 24 – Penalty Shot

The 'Spin-O-Rama' move, as described in Section 24.2 of the 2013-14 NHL Rule Book, will no longer be permitted either in Penalty Shot situations or in the Shootout.

Rule 38 – Video Goal Judge

Video review will be expanded in the following areas:

* Rule 38.4 (viii) has been modified to allow broader discretion to Hockey Operations to assist the referees in determining the legitimacy of all potential goals (e.g., to ensure they are "good hockey goals"). The revised Rule will allow Hockey Operations to correct a broader array of situations where video review clearly establishes that a "goal" or "no goal" call on the ice has been made in

error. The new expanded rule will also allow Hockey Operations to provide guidance to referees on goal and potential goal plays where the referee has blown his whistle (or intended to blow his whistle) after having lost sight of the puck.

* In reviewing "Kicked in Goals," Hockey Operations will require more demonstrable video evidence of a "distinct kicking motion" in order to overrule a "goal" call on the ice, or to uphold a "no goal" call on the ice.

Rule 57 – Tripping

The rule relating to "Tripping" will be revised to specifically provide that a two minute minor penalty will be assessed when a defending player "dives" and trips an attacking player with his body/arm/shoulder, regardless of whether the defending player is able to make initial contact with the puck.

But, in situations where a penalty shot might otherwise be appropriate, if the defending player "dives" and touches the puck first (before the trip), no penalty shot will be awarded. (In such cases, the resulting penalty will be limited to a two-minute minor penalty for tripping.)

Rule 64 – Diving / Embellishment

The supplementary discipline penalties associated with Rule 64.3 (Diving/Embellishment) will be revised to bring attention to and more seriously penalize players (and teams) who repeatedly dive and embellish in an attempt to draw penalties. Fines will be assessed to players and head coaches on a graduated scale outlined below.

2013 rule changes

All players with fewer than 25 games experience were required to wear visors.

The additional minor penalty for instigating a fight when wearing a visor was removed. Players were now assessed an extra minor penalty for unsportsmanlike conduct should they remove their helmet prior to fighting.

Jerseys which were not worn properly (such as being tucked in), and other equipment infractions would now result in a minor penalty.

The base of the goal frame was now shallower and narrower by 4 inches. The overall width of the base of the frame was reduced from 96 to 88 inches and the depth of the base of the frame was reduced from 44 to 40 inches. Additionally, the corners where the goal post meets the crossbar were bent with a smaller radius, allowing more area across the goal plane. The size of the goal itself remains 6 feet wide and 4 feet tall.

The attainable pass exception to the icing rule was removed. Officials would nullify a potential icing only if a player made contact with the puck.

A new hybrid icing rule was adopted. The hybrid icing rule required officials to stop play immediately in a potential icing situation where, in the judgement of the official, the defender would win a race to the puck ahead of an attacker, and the puck would cross the goal line. The official was to make his judgement when a player gains an imaginary line connecting the end-zone faceoff dots. Note that the first player to gain this imaginary line may not have been the one who would win a race to the puck.

Hybrid-icing rule changes. The League had been using the touch-icing system since 1937. Attainable pass rule wiped out — The NHL erased the attainable pass language from the icing rule, requiring officials to wave off icing only if a player touches the puck.

The attainable pass rule used to give the linesman discretion to determine if the pass could have been touched. If he felt it could have been he would wave off the icing.

Rule 48 changed: "A hit resulting in contact with an opponent's head where the head was the main point of contact and such contact to the head was avoidable is not permitted." The old rule included the words "targeted" and "principal point of contact."

Shallower nets:

Goalie equipment reduction - a goalie's leg pads can't go higher on his leg than 45 percent of the distance between the center of his knee and pelvis. The pads can go no higher than nine inches above the knee for goalies with an upper-leg measurement of 20 inches, which is roughly the average number for goalies in the NHL. The previous rule, which was instituted prior to the 2010-11 season, stated that leg pads could not go higher than 55 percent of the distance between the center of a goalie's knee and his pelvis, and that a goalie with a 20-inch upper-leg measurement could wear a pad that goes no higher than 11 inches above the center of his knee.

2017/18 season

If the coach challenges a play but is unsuccessful the challenging team will be charged a two minute penalty.

Those are some of the rule changes not all of them. It's a lot, isn't it? So in this 10 year period the NHL fundamentally changed. Redline is gone, offside changed, goalies can't play the puck outside of this weird area, nets are smaller behind, face off dot changes, offsides are changed, overtime changed, shootouts added. All in 10 or so years. It's a completely different game than hockey was previously.

It takes time for these new rules to take affect in the amateur ranks and to see it come to fruition at the professional ranks. I think we're just starting to see the valley of the talent lull entering the NHL due to these rule changes. None of this was necessary. Goaltender equipment got too big too fast and scoring disappeared. And instead of tackling the problem head on, those teams with good goalies and a defensive structure fought tooth and nail to prevent doing the obvious which was aggressively reducing goalie equipment size.

By going down these weird roads the game hockey ceased to exist. I don't know what it is now but it's not hockey as we knew it. The red line removal removed offensive opportunity. The blue line offside removed offensive opportunity. Stopping the goalie from playing the puck removed scoring chances. Making more room behind the net stopped scoring chances (you can't hide back there now, everyone can see you.) All of these things they thought they were doing to help - didn't.

Adding video review and coaches' challenges just prolonged the agony of watching a game. They couldn't just trust the referee? (Or two referees? Remember, they added a second referee in the 2000/01 season because presumably it was better than one so that the calls would be correct and then they reversed course on that and said they now need two referees AND video review AND a coaches' challenge.) Wouldn't it be great if it was just one referee and two linesman and they were in charge and everyone just behaved like adults and accepted their verdicts? I know. It's weird, eh? You could just have a game and a guy refereeing it and everyone accepted it as just a game and not life and death on a battlefield.

Whatever the state of the game the kids will adapt given time. And they will adapt to these changes for the worse. The game was stagnated before Bobby Orr arrived and he figured out a way to change it. The game was again stagnated but along came Wayne Gretzky and he changed the game again. If the NHL had just been patient, tackled goalie equipment and not tried to make all these drastic changes another player was coming to change the game. By continuing to move the goalposts from the kids you eliminate the kids who learned to overcome and adapt.

Every time you make a rule change it takes someone from the age of five to play with the new rule and adapt to it and overcome it. The best course of action is to keep it the same. What changed? Goalie equipment. How do you fix it? Change it back. Instead they ventured down this road of fundamentally altering the game which favours low talent fast skating players. Who benefits from removing a redline to try stretch passes? Really fast straight line skaters. Who benefits from the change in offsides? People who can chase the puck in a straight line. Speed skaters. Speed skaters are different than hockey players.

Where do scoring opportunities come from? Change of pace. If you're playing the game at 99 percent full throttle every shift where are you going to get the change of pace from? And so by drafting year after year based on speed they've removed a good portion of the kids who could have changed the pace. And by changing the rules you're eliminating those kids who were going to figure it out for you.

Was there a need for television review? In the Stanley Cup playoffs in 2017 there was a goal called back in the Finals that may have altered the Series. Nashville scored the first goal of game five but Pittsburgh challenged it and it was determined about 90 seconds previous to the goal a Nashville player entered the zone offside (although how you could tell from the video review is beyond me.) So they rolled the goal back and of course Pittsburgh then scores the first goal and Nashville loses by a goal. And you can still argue whether the Nashville player's foot was on the ice or not. So did it help to remove controversy? No of course it did not. All it did was delay the game and create more controversy. Who needs it? It's a complete waste of time.

And why are there two referees on the ice? Does anyone know? In the Finals same series, 2017, Nashville scored a goal but it was waved off because a referee, out of position, lost sight of the puck that was laying in the crease in front of an open net and was tapped in for a goal by Nashville. That also might have altered the Series but it was a blown call.

How many times in a game do we see a player run into a referee because the ref is in the way? It's a constant battle for the players to get past the referee in the offensive zone. There used to be just the one referee, usually out by the blue line, until the 2000/01 season when the commissioner added a second referee to make it like the NBA. I guess the theory was to crack down on infractions behind the play. I have to ask the question why? Part of the entertainment of hockey was the stuff that went on behind the play and usually only the people in the arena could see it because the TV audience would be following the play. This was the most exciting stuff in hockey. Spears and punches, boys being boys, when the ref wasn't watching. It was outstanding. It led to individual rivalries and was entertaining. Somewhere along the line this was forgotten. It's a game.

Does it really need video review? Why? Was there something wrong with a goal judge behind the net? When did it become so life and death to determine whether a goal is a goal or not that it's sent to a video room in Toronto? There's a referee on the ice. Does boxing stop its matches to determine if a punch landed or not? And like boxing there's nothing wrong with a tie.

And like boxing the referee can help the game or fight along.

It's a really important part of the game which has been forgotten here. The referee with the name on the back of the sweater is gone. Why? Because someone wanted to take the referees out of the show. And it's wrong, totally wrong. (And by the way why aren't there any women referees? It's not like it's required to be a male to use judgement. In fact, many people would argue women have better judgement anyways. They should be on the ice.) The single referee could control the pace of the game. If the game was sucking badly he (or she) could interject entertainment by calling a marginal penalty and that used to happen. The referee has to get something going here. That's entertainment. He could get a feel for the game by letting it go or clamping down. In a single referee game someone was in charge. In a two-referee system no one is in charge. They keep looking for the other person to do something.

And you have the absurdity of a referee 100 feet away from the play making calls because he thinks he sees some infraction the other referee isn't calling who is standing right beside the "infraction." It just turns into a mess. Not only are the referees constantly in the way they aren't controlling the game and they aren't adding entertainment value.

There was nothing better than going to a game and seeing a Kerry Fraser and knowing he was a terrible referee and booing him all night long and at the end of the game realize he'd done a good job, again. And his hair was perfect. And fans would get an affinity towards a referee. Which one would call a fair game for his or her team and which one was hated. It just added to the flavour of the game. Making them wear helmets hurt too but I understand it's a safety issue. These were the real stars of the game and putting the game back in their hands would definitely help the entertainment level.

All the yelling back and forth with the coaches was fantastic. And some referees had a short fuse and boy when it got lit look out! It was outstanding entertainment, a real show. This got lost somewhere in the desire to win games at all costs with video reviews and loser points and defense. The NHL is a Broadway show at heart. It's why we loved the game. The garbage cans being thrown on the ice or the sticks or the gum. The referees pointing the finger and yelling "You're out of here!" It was baseball right in the hockey rink. I can't stress enough how highly entertaining it was. Instead of nurturing this environment and paying these highly skilled individuals as part of the show, they continually battled them in negotiations and removed their names off their shirts. It was absolutely the wrong direction to go in. Boy are they missed in today's game. It's just not the same.

Hockey had umpires like MLB, physical contact like NFL, fights like boxing, sticks hitting or deflecting pucks like batting in MLB and passing like the NBA. Hockey had the whole nine yards. Why would you take that one aspect, umpiring, out of the game? The NFL still maintains the one head referee aspect and it sells the game. I worry MLB is going down the same road with the video reviews and "strike zone computer" garbage. Get it out of the game! My goodness. If we wanted a "perfect" game we could get robots to play it. It's the human element we love. It's the human element we hate. Get it wrong, get it right, should anyone really care? It's part of the entertainment.

Somehow somewhere the whole idea of playing sports got lost in the shuffle from the top to the bottom where the kids are playing. It's about fun, it's about athletics, it's about humanity moving towards perfection and it's about sportsmanship. Where did it go? This whole move to video reviews because people at home can see on tv a goal which wasn't called a goal at the game is just stupid. Who cares? What was the purpose of bending to the whims of the people whining in their living rooms that a called goal wasn't a goal - it didn't cross the line damn it! Not if the referee thought it did. That should be good enough. There was no need to go there. There's no need to back games up 90 seconds either because of an offside. What the hell is that?

The human element is why we watch. It's what we enjoy. We don't need computers and video film here. It's too serious. It's not enjoyable when people are so obsessed with a game they need to review the minute detail of every play. Put it back in the hands of the referee. Tell the coaches to throw stuff on the ice if they don't like the call. Get thrown out of the game. Give us entertainment. Give us a show.

These rule changes have led to vanilla hockey. Nowadays fans at an NHL game don't get up and lustily cheer after a goal is scored because they're not sure if it's going to be challenged or not. And if it's challenged then you've got anywhere from 60 to 300 seconds of sitting around, tapping your toes, watching the scoreboard, and then the disappointment if the goal is not a goal judged by someone 2,000 miles away. It just kills the spontaneity of the game and atmosphere. It's a game. It's not a science. It's not supposed to be exactly measured. It's art.

One of the rule changes I struggle with is the instigator rule introduced in 1992 which gives an additional penalty to someone who starts a fight (thus penalizing enforcers who policed the games.) I believe in fighting at the NHL level but I hate the idea of kids fighting in the AHL or in junior. I'm totally fine with it at the NHL level because they're adults and they get paid handsomely to do it and if they want to sign a waiver and agree to take the job I say it's a free North America, go and make money for your wife and kids.

It does serve a very good purpose at the NHL level. However, that being said, there has to be a way to get gloves under the gloves and take the bareknuckled aspect out of the fighting. I'm not a Don Cherry fan, usually, but I think he's right on this. The stars are getting run and hit on every shift without fear of repercussions. And let's face it, it's good entertainment IF and only IF the fighters are better protected perhaps with small MMA type gloves on and MMA style helmets on. If the helmets come off then the referees have to step right in.

Fighting is uncomfortable because we know there can be repercussions for some of these fighters. But a job is a job as far as I'm concerned. If they need to do this to take care of their wife and kids and they know straight up what the issues are afterwards for some of them, I think they have a right to work. They are adults. But I strongly disagree with it at the AHL level because they just don't make enough money doing it. I believe if a fight starts at the AHL level the linesmen and referee have to jump in right away. Don't let it go. Then the kids at the AHL level can show they have a temper but not have to go through too much pain. For $1 million per year I think it's ok for a man to say, that's how I'm going to support my family. For $50,000 per year it's not okay.

And at junior level the players should be tossed right away from the game. It's a skill development league and as such you want as many of those crop of 14-year-olds getting through to the age of 18 as possible and knowing they're not going to fight in hockey is a good start. If someone wants to make a career in hockey as a fighter they can also take another sport such as boxing and use it as a statement about where they'd like to specialize as an NHL player. Boxing will teach them valuable skills to defending their heads as well.

The NHL should approach rule changes from above the GM's level only. It's an ownership decision to fundamentally change the product they bought. I understand they appoint the GM but they also fire the GM and so there's too much change and bickering at this level and not enough looking at the whole of the game.

The rules of the last 20 years should be tossed except for the goalie equipment changes. And all they need to really do is keep reducing goalie equipment sizes until they get the goal scoring they want. It's not really complicated. It doesn't have to include fundamental changes to the game.

COST OF HOCKEY

This is the biggest problem for the NHL because we're not seeing athletes from across the political and socio-economic spectrum enter the game. For the most part, hockey is for rich kids. It's an upsetting statement, and not 100% correct in all cases, but it's an accurate statement. And if you're not getting the poor kids involved in your sport you're not getting the complete athlete in your sport. Period. End of story. Hockey has moved out of the reach of most middle class families as well. So who's playing it? Well-heeled people that's for sure. It's also not a 100 percent accurate statement for everyone in the NHL. I'm sure there are some people in the game familiar with welfare or food stamps. But it's a precious small amount who understand the concept of fighting for food everyday.

I'll make some generalizations but they're common sense generalizations. Boys with younger dads are tougher than those with older dads because the dad is stronger and brasher. But one thing older dads usually have is money. And so what hockey gets are the sons of men whose testosterone left a couple of decades ago. And while it might be good if you're raising children intended for left-wing universities it doesn't work as well as young dads making athletes. Testosterone is a hormone which controls sex drive, regulates sperm production, promotes muscle mass, increases energy, and even influences human behaviour (such as aggression and competitiveness.) As men get older they lose testosterone. Past the age of 30 men lose one percent per year. So by 40 they have lost 10 percent of this power hormone. At 50 it's a 20 or more percent loss. If an engine were to lose 20 percent of it's compression, you'd be pulling it and rebuilding it.

And so what you can conclude is sons whose fathers are in their 20s have a much more powerful dad. Louder, stronger, prone to emotional outbursts - they are full-blown males. But they usually don't have the money as someone in their fifties. And so they are generally poor households where hockey isn't going to be an option. Ball hockey would be an option or basketball or football or just being out on the street getting into trouble. These are the risk takers. These are the kids who you want in your programs especially hockey. These are the ones who learn to fight. They're stronger, meaner, tougher and are usually more physically active than those in upper-middle class households. Again, this is a generalization and not true for 100 percent of the kids in upper-class homes.

The point I'm trying to make is kids from lower income households are rougher around the edges. I live in a lower income neighbourhood with the best high-school football program, pound for pound, in Canada. It's a tough area with tough kids. And they love their football and rugby. They love to hit and fight and get in the trenches and pound people. They have earned a mean, nasty reputation. And because it's put on through the high-school it's an affordable thing for them. The same school has just terrific basketball players. They get after it. And I'll be honest, their grade 12 team is pretty frightening to look at. Getting on the court against them is all the demonstration of courage you need. And there's a lot of First Nation kids in these programs. And they're good. And they're tough. Damned tough.

The same area produces a lacrosse team that punches way above it's weight. It's the same program that produced John Ferguson, the Montreal Canadiens great from Vancouver who played lacrosse in Nanaimo. This is his bio from wikipedia. This is exactly what I'm talking about.

"Ferguson was born in Vancouver, British Columbia on September 5, 1938. His father died when he was nine and he was raised by his mother near the Pacific National Exhibition grounds. Ferguson loved horses and hung around Hastings Park as a child. Aside from his interest in horses and hockey he also played lacrosse. Ferguson's hockey career began as a stickboy for the Vancouver Canucks, then of the Western Hockey League. He became interested in the role of enforcer when he saw the more talented Canucks players get hit repeatedly without having their team-mates attempt to respond or dissuade their opponents."

Ferguson is the type of man you want in the NHL. I don't think there's any chance because of money constraints he would have made the NHL in 2016.

Have you ever wondered why, in a country with so many First Nations, there's never been more than a handful of them make it to the NHL? I think it's about money. Plain and simple. And so hockey costs so much it is not an option for a lot of First Nations kids. Not all but a lot. There's also a cultural and racism factor for them to overcome. I'm not sure we create an environment for ensuring they join and continue in hockey. Again, getting back to the leaving home at 14 issue, for a lot of First Nations, that's unthinkable because of family bonds. But there is racism too. I read a news story lately about a First Nations mom who sent her child to a high-school in Thunder Bay looking for a better future. The young man didn't make any friends and went to a theatre, alone, and when he came out he was attacked by some white kids because he was Indian. And they beat him to the point where he jumped into a near frozen river and swam across and climbed out, miraculously, and got to his dorm and called his mom who drove all night to go and bring him home. Talk about tough. He would have made one hell of a hockey player.

When I was 15 I had a lot of friends on my team who were First Nations. And we were playing a team from Port Hardy and things got heated on the ice, as they usually did, for our First Nations kids. They were clearly targets during the games. And after the game some of the kids who were part of the kickboxing team from Port Hardy came in with their coach into our dressing room and the coach locked the door. (We didn't have a coach for most of the time.) And they proceeded to beat the living shit out of three of our First Nations players inside the dressing room. And I'm not proud to admit I did nothing. I, along with the other white kids I think, had never seen this kind of violence before. And I'm proud to say our First Nations kids gave one hell of a fight. But I was 15 and 170 pounds and scared crapless and I never got in the fight. None of us did anything to help. It was all over in 90 seconds and of course the grown man in the dressing room locking the door and guarding it and staring at us rooted us to our seats. I get angry about this from time to time. Kevin Wasden was one of the kids on our team from Alert Bay and he was exceptional and could have made the NHL or at least the AHL. And Kevin died in a truck accident and I believe he was 20. I never got the chance to say I'm sorry Kevin. He asked me after the fight, bleeding, why didn't I do anything? I never said anything but just stood there looking at the blood on his face. I don't think any of us ever said anything after that. Anyways, it's stuck with me for a long time. All for the colour of their skin. And so when I say First Nations kids are tough, they're tough, they have to be tough in ways white people don't.

And so kids from tougher socio-economic backgrounds have an uphill climb if they want to play hockey. It's easily $10,000 per year for the rep teams, the travel and more for the summer camps. Where would you even come up with that kind of money? And so the majority of parents steer their children clear of hockey I think in most part because of the enormous cost involvement. Full disclosure for honesty purposes I went to Howie Meeker's summer schools and to the Penticton Knights camp. However, the cost back then was a few hundred dollars and was a place for my parents to dump me while they were at the beach (good parenting move though!) I'm talking about camps costing thousands of dollars not a couple of hours per day on ice. It's grown immensely in 40 years.

The number one sport in Canada in terms of children enrolled is swimming with over 1,000,000 kids enrolled. Soccer is second with over 750,000. Dance is third at 600,000 and hockey is fourth at 500,000. Most parents I know think it's foolish to even consider ice hockey. So what you see at the NHL level, for the most part, there are exceptions of course, is rich kids. They are kids from rich households or at least upper middle class. It's not the best crop of genes to select athletes from. And I'm sorry, again, it's a generalization but in my opinion it's a correct one.

Poor kids learn to take a punch. They learn to go without dinner. They get tougher. They get meaner. And their release is usually sports. They don't have the latest XBox or internet or other time wasters. They have a stick and a tennis ball and a road or a school wall and they're there for hours just smacking the ball around. Or inside the gym or in the playground shooting hoops for hours at a time. These are the gym rats. The rink rats. The playground rats. These are the true athletes. These are the ones that hone their hand-eye coordination from birth. These are the ones outside from dusk to dawn and go screw your homework, I'm not interested. They come primarily from lower middle class and poor families and that makes up the majority of Canadian households. And no amount of weight-training or hockey studying will make up for what these kids have which is genetically hardwired into them.

And it's even more pronounced now than it was 30 years ago because of the income divide between poor and rich. And 40 years ago there weren't computers or Xboxes or even cable tv where I grew up. There was outside on the street from dusk til dawn playing. But now these poor kids barely get outside. And so ice hockey kids are put in safe programs at what is an enormous fee. It's so much money it's hard to fathom. I hope you're sitting down for this. The hockey academies that kids are pressured into attending to become "elite" hockey players can cost as much as $35,000 to $50,000 per summer. I can't even imagine coming up with that kind of money to spend on a child's game. I don't know how anyone gets from here to there. That's a university degree in one summer paid for, signed, sealed and delivered for your child. But some parents spend it on gambling at the race track, which is essentially what it is thinking their child will make it to the NHL. Only .1 percent of them will make it.

Some parents at the time of the draft may have $500,000 invested in their child. It's stunning, just stunning. That's a second house, a cottage on the lake, a retirement. And where is the Canadian government in this stepping in and stopping this madness? There are so many of these "camps" trying to turn kids into pro-athletes. Hey, I don't blame ex-NHLers or other people from holding these camps. I think they do it for the best of intentions and for money obviously and Canada and the United States are free countries. But somewhere along the line the big picture is lost. Someone has to step in and take a big picture view and discourage this practice.

It's ridiculous to think it will help too. All it takes is a stick, a tennis ball, a jug of water, some sandwiches and a kick out the door by the parents. There's no need for this. You've probably heard the saying it takes 10,000 hours to master something. It's especially true in hockey. It doesn't matter how the hours are accumulated.

The peer pressure it puts on other parents is a factor too. Little Johnny next door is going to the summer camp for elite hockey players so our son has to go to keep up. And my goodness. What in the hell people. What in the hell. What are you doing? And again, no one is doing this to harm the kids or with bad intentions. It just spiralled out of hand to the point of insanity.

And as you can see with that kind of price tag, you can forget the vast majority of kids playing hockey for a living and if you want to see the best Canadian athletes they likely won't be in hockey. In fact if you look at Canada's basketball program you'll see all the evidence you need to see I'm correct. Canada may now have the second best basketball program in the world and in the near future be second only to the United States in delivering players to the NBA. How'd you like them apples? Soccer is a different kettle of fish. Canada may improve drastically in soccer and make absolutely no dent in world rankings because it's a very small country and everyone plays soccer.

Hockey enrolment has been declining while girl's enrolment in hockey has been increasing, meaning even fewer boys are playing hockey. What you're seeing at the NHL are for the most part manufactured hockey players. People with deep pockets who spent oodles of money on a kid to produce an NHL player. Thus the robotic nature of hockey today.

DRAFT LOTTERY

I won't spend a lot of time on this other than to say it contributes to why the NHL sucks right now. First off there's a ridiculous formula to come up with who drafts what and where. And it wasn't necessary. The draft was changed because teams were tanking on purpose to get a franchise player they knew was coming down the pipeline. For example you could argue the Penguins did it twice; once for Lemieux, once for Crosby. The Leafs jettisoned players to get Auston Matthews. And the Edmonton Oilers appeared to be in no hurry to win games with McDavid coming down the pipeline when they won him in the lottery. And there's nothing wrong with it in my opinion.

It was the Oilers who really got everyone's dander up when they continually ended up with the first overall pick. In 2015 the NHL changed the lottery giving the 10 highest-finishing non-playoff qualifying teams better odds of getting first overall pick and of course they took those odds from the four lowest finishing teams. Now the four worst teams in the NHL have virtually no chance of getting first overall pick (except somehow the Toronto Maple Leafs pulled off the feat so it can happen.) It was a really simple fix to stop the Edmonton Oilers from continually getting a first overall pick. All the NHL had to do was ban teams from getting the first overall pick for five years once they got it. So for example, now the New Jersey Devils, who got the first overall pick in 2017 draft won't be eligible for the first overall pick until 2023. It's nice and simple. Yes, you could add a bit of weight to the lottery, for example the team that finishes last right now has the best chance of picking fourth in the draft. That's wrong. It should be about an 80 percent chance of picking first. But a slight possibility of dropping to second and no further. The team that finishes second worse in the regular season should pick no worse than third and have a 15 percent chance of going to first overall. The point is you can tank, get the first overall pick but you're not doing it again. You're gone. And so everyone starts to share the first overall pick.

But the NHL has kept tinkering with the draft lottery until teams can't rebuild in the draft anymore. There's no rhyme or reason to it with the way they have it weighted. For example, the Vancouver Canucks finished 29th out of 30 teams and picked fifth overall and didn't get any help in the draft. The player they selected was a gamble and one who might play in four to five years, as in most NHL drafts, after the first two draft picks, well... good luck with that! In any given NHL draft there really are only a couple of players who can help right away. Those picks should go to the worst teams so their fan bases know they're going to get help. And they should also know once they get their pick, they're out of the first overall draft for five years.

And again, the draft lottery changes in 2015 impacted what team? The Vancouver Canucks square in the face. They continually fall in the NHL draft and are unlikely to get help from the draft for many years to come. And the other team which is hurt from this system is the Buffalo Sabres. They were slated to pick Connor McDavid... and fell to second pick. Yes the Sabres tried to help their draft position, or tank, but who cares? The

Buffalo Sabres have been in the league for 47 years, shouldn't they have received McDavid?

Tanking should be a strategy for GMs. It's also fun for fans to follow. But again, with the rule change I suggested, you're not going to get the Oilers sitting at the first overall pick over and over again. They get booted out. Now they need to make sure New Jersey is booted out for several years. By doing this you start changing the odds of the other teams requiring help in the lottery, eventually you'll always have five teams prevented from the first overall pick and I would consider preventing them from a top three pick as well in those years. But if it's too draconian I yield the argument on the top three pick. Eventually you'd always get the right teams getting draft help. Right now you have fans in cities tuning the NHL out now because why would you bother? They sit through entire seasons of garbage and get no help in the draft. The current system is going to create cycles of decades of losing for teams.

PLAYOFFS

What on Earth is going on in the playoffs? They're called by the referees in a completely different manner than the regular season and it's played at a different speed by the players than the regular season. It's too much of a jump from one place to another. In the NFL a penalty in game one of the season is a penalty in the Super Bowl. But in the NHL the further a team advances in the playoffs the more it becomes a rodeo on the ice because the refereeing changes. You see infractions in the Finals which were called in another game earlier in the regular season or even earlier in the playoffs. There's no consistency from one season to the next or series to series or even game to game. And I'm not blaming the NHL or the referees. There's a ton of pressure on them to "let it go!" from the media. There is a culture in the NHL, which I think is a natural part of being a human being, of not wanting to become the show especially as games become more and more important as the playoffs continue. It's a really hard job for both NHL and referees and clearly they're doing the best they can. But there's one simple way to fix it: call everything in the book and don't use "judgement."

The two-referee system doesn't help because no one is in charge. If one referee is letting something go then it's human nature for the other referee to also let it go to be a part of a team. And so little by little the games degenerate. And then you get a rodeo and then you had Trap teams make full comebacks with the Ottawa Senators getting to the Conference Finals in 2017 despite numerous injuries playing a full-on Trap which was supposedly eliminated because of the removal of the red line. Not quite it would seem.

If you're a casual fan or not a fan of the teams involved there has to be something exciting about the game in order to watch. There was nothing in the 2017 playoffs even remotely interesting. Malkin led the playoffs with points and at times he took over games. And he was able to take the pressure off his teammates to achieve victory but it wasn't fun to watch. Malkin used brute strength to get his team the Stanley Cup and the Nashville Predators were too small to respond. There was nothing else. The Penguins used two goalies. None of the games had suspense. I watched the NBA Finals instead and I hate the NBA. But the Cleveland Cavaliers and Golden State Warriors Finals was so compelling I bought in. There were games of absolute futility in the NHL. Players struggled to make 20 foot passes. The puck would bounce off of their sticks, then they would chase the puck to the corner, dump it out, chase the puck again. I kept thinking to myself are these actually professional hockey players? Is this as good as it gets? One would hope not. To fall from the grace and magic of the 1994 Stanley Cup Finals to what was served up as hockey in 2017 is stunning. It's only been 23 years since New York.

Another problem with the playoffs is the format. Everything humanely possible must be done to get No. 1 seeds to the Finals. They should get a first round bye and extra games at home in a seven game series perhaps five at home and two on the road and I would go as far as letting them choose their opponents. There's nothing worse than an eight place seed squeaking into the playoffs and starting the rodeo and getting to the Finals or worse, winning it. And by rodeo I mean the hooking and holding and lassoing of opponents. I saw a clothesline delivered in the playoffs in 2017 and taking the cake of stupidity was Toronto Maple Leafs Nazem Kadri blatantly taking a run at Washington Capitals star Alexander Ovechkin's knees. It finished Ovechkin's run in the playoffs for all intents and purposes. Kadri wasn't suspended for taking out the game's best player and he said he wasn't aiming at Ovechkin's knees. Even if you take Kadri at his word then he still accidentally targeted the knees of the best player on the best team in the playoffs.

The reason you want to prevent eighth place teams from proceeding is because they invariably play a terrible brand of hockey to get there. The frontrunners usually play a more pleasing style of game. And because you should want to even out the regular season and playoff play then you need to eliminate these lower teams.

And if there are suspensions in the playoffs they're bizarre to say the least. In 2011 Vancouver Canucks defenseman Aaron Rome got the longest suspension in NHL history with a four game suspension in the Finals for a perfectly legal hit which in the league's eyes was deemed late. (NHL values Finals suspensions as equivalent to seven regular season games, so it was the equivalent of 28 games for Rome and the Canucks.) In 2017 Columbus Blue Jackets forward Matt Calvert was suspended one game for breaking his stick across the face of a Penguin and then turning around and hitting him in the head to the ice for good measure. Rome's hit was a hockey play, Calvert's play, while funny and entertaining, wasn't.

And then you compound the problem with things like in 2011 the son of the NHL's disciplinary boss playing for the Boston Bruins, recusing himself for the Finals (why just the Finals?) and handing control of the suspensions to his good friend who proceeded to hammer Rome with an enormous suspension. I'm sure there was no malice intended towards Vancouver. I think they tried to get it right. However, the appearance of a conflict of interest is often as equal to the actual conflict of interest. A neutral third party outside the NHL disciplinary circle might have been a better solution. There was a riot after those Finals in Vancouver with millions of dollars in damages and hundreds of arrests. Can they be linked to fans feelings of injustice? Maybe. Maybe not. But in any case violence is never a solution to anything especially since it's just a game. But it does show you the emotions people invest in their teams and when emotions are involved clear thinking is not.

Interest in playoffs should build as the playoffs go forward. But in hockey it's the opposite. The first round is the best round of hockey and it's downhill from there. There were empty seats in 2017 for the Anaheim Ducks games and Ottawa Senators games so interest wanes in both Canada and America. The NBA is the exact opposite. The excitement builds to the Finals. I think the NHL has to try to get more of the NBA in its playoffs (not the pre-ordained bit) but at least try to make it more of a national interest and not a regional interest. Consistency between the rules of the regular season and the playoffs is a must. And turning over all league supplementary discipline decisions to a neutral third party would certainly turn down the temperature.

TORONTO INFLUENCE

There's too much Toronto in the NHL. Head office, hall of fame, war room and TV rights owner are all located there. Yes, Toronto is the biggest city in Canada. Okay, but so what? Half of America couldn't find it on a map and the rest of Canada hates it with a passion. There's no historic basis for any of these things to be in Toronto other than they are in Toronto which was York and changed it's name to Toronto. Windsor, Nova Scotia is generally regarded as the birthplace of hockey in Canada. Montreal was the first city to host actual hockey games. New Westminster, B.C. was instrumental in the founding of Hockey Canada and the Allan Cup. Vancouver was the largest venue for hockey up to the 1920s. My point being what made Toronto special to get everything?

Stanley Park is in Vancouver, British Columbia. The trophy given by Lord Stanley to Canada was awarded to the NHL in 1947 despite the fact the Pacific Coast Hockey Association, which became the Western Hockey League, was still going. And so every year the NHL hands out a trophy from Toronto which was won for the NHL "de facto" while Western Canada still continued its professional hockey using the Lester Patrick Cup until 1974, which is also, for some bizarre reason, located in

Toronto. The Stanley Cup wasn't the unanimous award for hockey championships even across Canada, other than the NHL was on the CBC (headquartered in Toronto) and nobody else was (even though people in B.C. were funding the CBC, and therefore the NHL, indirectly.)

I'm not saying the NHL wasn't better than the other leagues what I'm saying is there was a rival league in Canada headquartered in B.C. because there were no jet planes. There wasn't jet travel the way there is today. So there had to be two distinct leagues because there was no way to get from Los Angeles to Montreal other than a very long train ride over seven days. So it wasn't practical for the two leagues to play.

The NHL itself hasn't been a unique league for very long. It had a rival, located in Vancouver existing right up until 1974. It had teams in San Francisco, Denver, Seattle, Portland, Victoria, New Westminster, Calgary, Los Angeles and Edmonton to name just a few. It was quite a going concern. Even Don Cherry played in the league. Trades were completed between the two leagues.

NHL star Andy Bathgate purposefully left the NHL to join the NHL's rival, the WHL Vancouver Canucks in 1969 and 1970 to win two consecutive Lester Patrick Cups. He returned to the NHL in 1971. And then there's the World Hockey Association which also ran briefly as a competitor to the NHL from 1972 to 1979. (The WHL was a direct competitor from 1952 to 1974.) And so my point is hockey existed right across North America in professional leagues. But the ability to fly across North America wasn't invented yet. The Boeing 727 jet airliner started flying in 1962 and NHL expansion came in 1967.

And so what is the reason all of the powers of the NHL are located in Toronto? Why not Cleveland? St. Louis? They were a part of the original NHL. Of course the "official" headquarters were moved from Montreal to New York in 1989 but the actual headquarters of the operations is still located in Toronto on Bay Street. It wasn't closed. And with the addition of video reviews from an office in Toronto it's gained even more power. At one time there was a head office in Montreal where the NHL was founded so wouldn't it make more sense to have the head office back in Montreal where it has a link to history?

With the NHL being a regional sport in Canada, with one NHL city despising another with a passion, why would you locate something as inflammatory as the "war room" to do video reviews in Toronto? How is it received by fans in Calgary when a Calgary goal against Toronto in Calgary is sent for review in Toronto and overturned? Probably not well. And it's even a worse situation in Vancouver which was the headquarters of the rival league and many people still remember it to be thus. Something like the video review office, which should be eliminated, but if they're keeping it put it in Los Angeles where they do this kind of work best and they're on a west coast time zone meaning they're not video reviewing at 3am. It doesn't make any sense whatsoever to have it in Toronto.

Then you couple this issue with Canadian media conglomerate Rogers owning the TV contract for the NHL. They paid $5.2 billion for a 12 year deal. Previously the CBC had held the rights for decades and it operated as a neutral third party because it was taxpayer owned. Rogers also owns a substantial stake in the Toronto Maple Leafs. Is it not bad enough Canada's national flag is the Toronto Maple Leafs uniform but in red and white? It would be like the United States adopting the New York Yankees symbol instead of the Stars and Stripes. Of course they voted on the flag in the 1960s before British Columbia and the west could even mount a resistance to Toronto taking over yet another Canadian thing. But that's a book for another time.

And so Rogers has a massive influence on the NHL by buying $5.2 billion of it. Now, it's complete crap but there are people who wear tinfoil hats who believe Rogers/Toronto Maple Leafs were awarded the first overall pick, Auston Matthews, very soon after buying the TV contract. It's not possible for the NHL to have rigged a lottery to help Toronto. I'm not even sure how anybody would or could rig it and then keep it quiet and how it would be okay with the other owners. It doesn't make sense. But just the fact the perception exists on places such as social media should concern the NHL. And the longer the TV contract goes the more the hatred for the game will build because more often than not a Canadian fan's team isn't going to win the Stanley Cup and they're going to start pointing fingers and turning off from the game they perceive to be crooked, even if it isn't. And if Toronto wins a Stanley Cup there will be many people believing Toronto bought the Stanley Cup through the purchase of the TV contract with its parent company. I don't believe for one second it's even possible to buy a game because it is a game. However, the perception because of the ownership connection to the NHL is real.

I haven't seen much pushback from the NHL to convince tinfoil wearing conspiracist Canadians everything is above board. And there should be a great effort to do this even if only to appease nutbars. It could start by shuttering it's offices located in Toronto and moving to somewhere like Los Angeles. It would kill the perception from some fans the head of Rogers is walking around the NHL's Toronto head office.

Since a lot of the sponsors of the NHL have head offices located in Toronto it may be difficult, even unwise, for them to completely shutter their offices. They could leave a sales office in Toronto but make it clear to everyone it's just a sales office. With emails and video conferencing it's possible to locate a head office anywhere and stay in touch in Toronto. It's a formality only but it's an important one.

Why are Hall of Fame induction ceremonies held in the Toronto arena? Does anyone know how that got hijacked? Again, Toronto is not a historic hockey place. Kingston, Ontario might be, but so is Nova Scotia and Montreal and Vancouver. Why is it Toronto? Why would the Sedins from Vancouver be honoured to be blessed by the fans in Toronto when they're inducted into the Hall-of-fame? Why wouldn't their Hall of Fame induction be held in somewhere meaningful to them rather than one which makes most in Vancouver vomit?

The official Hockey Hall of Fame should be moved to Windsor, Nova Scotia from Toronto. The NHL should construct an outdoor arena in Windsor and every year one NHL game should be played there with the Hall of Fame members, past and present attending with that year's inductees at the game in front of the original inventors of the game. And their statues should be put in a Hall of Fame in Windsor and it should be a pilgrimage for all hockey fans to visit the little town. But instead Toronto has the Hall of Fame.

Then there's Hall of Fame voting. They have 18 members on the selection committee and I can't find a single one of them in the Pacific Time Zone (there might be but I can't see one). This diminishes the Hall of Fame if you have 18 guys, mainly from Eastern Canada, doing the voting. It should be one vote per NHL city and no "hockey insiders." There should also be a season ticket holder component. The way they have it set up now is perplexing. That's not to suggest Hall of Fame voters and bosses are bad people and don't try their best or do a good job. Pat Quinn was the head of the Hall of Fame voting committee for a time and his heart was always in Vancouver no matter where he went and I think everyone can agree he was about as decent a human being as exists. But I think even the staunchest supporter of the current system has to see the flaws inherent in having the majority of voters from one area of the hockey world. By widening the voting field you create acceptance throughout Canada and the United States.

The trophy voting is even more of a puzzle. The Professional Hockey Writers Association votes on seven National Hockey League (NHL) individual awards: Hart Memorial Trophy, Lady Byng Memorial Trophy, Calder Memorial Trophy, James Norris Memorial Trophy, Conn Smythe Trophy, Bill Masterton Memorial Trophy, and Frank J. Selke Trophy. There are two people listed on the HWA as being from the pacific time zone. Only two. The vast majority are from, wait for it, Toronto. So what do you think happens on this voting? I'm sure they try to be unbiased but people do what they know and I can look at award winners and see the majority of the award winners are from the eastern time zone. It's probably not on purpose but if you live in the east and you see mainly eastern teams you have to be more comfortable voting for players you saw rather than ones you didn't. Some have even admitted they're fast asleep when games in the Western Conference are taking place. If you think about it for a minute, because of the way the planet turns and when the games are on TV, it makes more sense for these awards and hall of fames to be voted on by people from the Pacific Time Zone because they see all the games.

What was also odd was when the Eastern and Western Conferences didn't play each other and guess who won the majority of awards? From 2003 to 2012 the schedule was not balanced. But they didn't divide the awards having an MVP from the Eastern Conference and one from the Western Conference similar to MLB. Since 1991 in the Hart Trophy voting when Mark Messier of the New York Rangers won it to 2014/15 season when Montreal Canadien's Carey Price won it, 17 of the 23 winners were from the Eastern Conference.

From the 1991 season to the 2014/15 season the Norris Trophy has been won by Eastern time zone players a staggering 19 of 23 times. Now I freely admit some of these wins are completely legitimate from very good players who were in the eastern time zone. But holy cow, folks. It's a 75 percent chance the winners of most awards will be from the eastern time zone. Take that to Vegas.

Now, true, there are more teams in the eastern time zones but come on now. Eighty percent batting average? Is it critical to fixing the game? No, it's not really. But if you're going to bother to hand out awards then it should be as impartial as possible and the NHL should be examining this because it reflects upon them. They should change it to become more equitable as soon as possible. Their names are on the awards along with some very historic NHL figures. And they should NOT change the names of the trophies. It's history, leave it alone.

And it does affect things like the history books and Hall of Fame voting. Where does Sidney Crosby place in the standings as an all time great? I don't know. He's won two Conn Smythe Trophies which is in immediate dispute. He was behind both Phil Kessel and Evegni Malkin on his own team for goals and points the two years he won it. The Penguins don't win a Stanley Cup without their star goaltender Matt Murray who was the reason they won the Cup in 2016. And who can argue with what Malkin did in the entirety of 2017? Or was it Murray again saving their bacon?

But Crosby only scored eight goals in 24 games in 2017 and won the Conn Smythe, miraculously. He's a Toronto media darling and the voting is primarily done by Toronto media so what role did that play in the voting? And that could lead to Hall of Fame voting from the people in the same area. People outside of the Toronto area regard last year's inductee such as Dave Andreychuk or years previous Doug Gilmour, perhaps differently than those in Toronto, where both played for the Toronto Maple Leafs. I think most people outside of the market raised their eyebrows at both inductions. They were never regarded as top 5 players in their era. So it raises questions. Moving the Hall of Fame to a neutral site would help end this speculation.

Recent trophy winners baffle ones mind. Erik Karlsson in Ottawa has as many Norris Trophies as Hall of Fame shoe-in Duncan Keith. P.K. Subban, of Toronto, won a Norris Trophy playing in Montreal. Carey Price of the Montreal Canadiens won a Hart Trophy but Duncan Keith has no Hart Trophies and has only one more Norris Trophy than Subban.

It doesn't make sense. Keith anchored two Gold Medal teams and three Stanley Cups and is a top 25 player of all time. And Price has a Hart Trophy and he doesn't? You know who else did this? Jose Theodore also of the Montreal Canadiens. He won the Hart Trophy and Vezina Trophy in the same year, just like Carey Price. The only explanation I can come up with is the centralized media voting within these Toronto and Montreal markets creates group thinking. They see Theodore or Price or Subban every night, because they cover the beat every night, and so they start to myopically focus in on their beat and less on the rest of the league.

In 2011 Daniel Sedin of the Vancouver Canucks was a plus 30, had 41 goals and 104 points to win the Art Ross Trophy (most points in the NHL) and led his team to first on the power play, first on penalty killing and a Presidents Trophy for finishing first in the NHL. And Corey Perry who scored 50 goals and was a plus 9 on the 25th place team in the NHL won the Hart Trophy. Are you kidding? I can only assume the voters didn't want back-to-back Sedins from Sweden/Vancouver to win it rather they wanted the guy from Peterborough, Ontario, to have it. Yes, Perry had a good year. But his team finished 25th out of 30 teams, a mere 31 points behind the Canucks. There is no possible way Perry had any impact on his team close to Daniel Sedin because there were only five teams worse than his. Sedin's team was historical being the first team to be first on the power play and first on the penalty kill since the Montreal Canadiens of the mid-1970s. They gave the Hart Trophy to a last placed player as opposed to a first place player. Think about that.

The awarding of trophies shouldn't make fans laugh hysterically. And I'm not talking laughing at the award night ceremonies. And those also should be changed because they're silly. There's no meaning to them right now other than to provide comedy. Okay, so maybe I will change my mind. If the award ceremony is going to be funny then why not make the awards a joke too? Come on folks. If you're going to have an award ceremony then have the hockey greats from the 1950s and 1960s award the hardware. This should be a time for hockey fans to see the greats before they pass away and to pass history and culture on to the next generation.

ORIGINAL SIX

And so while continuing the prior chapter on too much Toronto it brings up the issue of the "Original Six" garbage which is perpetuated on the NHL teams not in the "Original Six" cities. It's pumped every single year by every single hockey media type from Toronto over and over again ad nauseam. First off, it's incorrect. The Detroit Red Wings are the Victoria Cougars of Victoria, British Columbia of the Pacific Coast Hockey Association and they were called the Detroit Cougars. They were sold to Detroit by the PCHA based in Vancouver. And the Chicago Blackhawks are the Portland Rosebuds of Oregon State who also played in the PCHA and was also sold by Vancouver. So if they're "original" why are they from Vancouver's hockey league and why are they NHL expansion teams? Pittsburgh and Ottawa were in the NHL in 1926. Other cities have been in the NHL prior to World War Two. St. Louis Eagles were in the NHL in 1938, why aren't they an "original" team?

And if the term suggests it was the only pro-hockey league in North America after World War II to 1967 that's also incorrect. There was a second pro-league awarding a championship yearly in western North America located in Vancouver called the WHL. There wasn't travel like there is today. It's a 25 year period of the NHL where they travelled by train existing with two donor expansion teams from Vancouver's league.

What's the objective here?

Is the purpose here just to humiliate Vancouver as much as possible or the entire rest of the league? The NHL is 100 years old but let's randomly celebrate just 25 years of it. They were way better than any other years. Does it make any sense? Do you hear anyone on the national tv broadcasts saying in a game between the Los Angeles Monarchs (Kings) and the Vancouver Canucks "here's a fantastic Western Hockey League rematch?" Why isn't that celebrated?

I think one of the reasons why the NHL isn't considered among the Big Three sports in the USA is because it's just so Toronto focused because they are one of the "original" six 25 year period of half of two countries. It's not big league. They don't celebrate its true North American history. They only focus on two Canadian cities and two American cities (two aren't legitimately original.) It is without question the stupidest thing in sports and that includes the annual tomato fight in Portugal.

Toronto continually seeks America's praise as an area of human accumulation. A city like Vancouver doesn't face the same issue as nearby large centres and so it doesn't constantly look for American approval. Why would it? Vancouver is a world class city. It doesn't need anyone's permission to exist as such. So I think "original six" is a manifestation of this inferiority complex encompassing Toronto. It's not ever going to be a world class destination city. So what? It's a large metropolitan area such as Cleveland or Detroit and there's nothing wrong with it. Not every city can be a Los Angeles, New York or Vancouver. And it's because of where they're located.

And from a financial aspect it's hurting the game because of all the media focus in Toronto and on

Toronto. A San Jose / Los Angeles game is business wise way more important than Toronto / Montreal but it's promoted as less meaningful even though they've got two Stanley Cups between them in the past 10 years. San Francisco and Los Angeles played each other in the Pacific Coast Hockey League in the 1940s, 80 years ago. Los Angeles has had professional hockey for decades and decades back to the 1940s and played San Francisco and Vancouver. There were teams in Fresno, Hollywood and Pasadena. You think the people of Los Angeles are unaware of this? And so media types supposedly promoting the NHL keep rubbing "Original Six" in their faces then wonder why ratings suck. Yes, I guess historically hockey in Ontario goes back to the 1800s. But Los Angeles was founded in 1781 and is a world class city. You really want to brag about history with a city like Los Angeles?

Edmonton and Vancouver have played against each other in professional hockey for almost as many decades as Toronto / Montreal. They go back to the 1930s. There might even be film footage of them playing. If it were promoted as more than just WHA expansion team verse NHL expansion team it might draw more money in and more viewers.

This incessant pandering towards Toronto's ego does nothing to celebrate and grow the game of hockey or the NHL and it serves no one any good. It's self-defeating and petty. Why doesn't the NHL step in and put a stop to it? It would never happen in the NFL or MLB or NBA. Here's an original American Football League matchup of the Buffalo Bills and the Denver Broncos on Monday Night Football! No, that doesn't happen. The league has to grow up and leave the nonsense behind.

Furthermore, Vancouver and Los Angeles should be designated NHL heritage cities and commemorated and celebrated to the detriment of the "original six." If you want to grow the game you need bigger pulls in the west. And the NHL has them for goodness sakes. The NHL is more than Ontario and it's more than 25 years old. The only good things to come out of the sixties were Jimi Hendrix, Janis Joplin, the Doors, the Beatles, Led Zeppelin, Canned Heat, Neil Young and the Rolling Stones and they're about 100x better than the "Original Six." And if you're going to navel gaze then embrace all of hockey's history by celebrating the PCHL and PCHA. Move forward and stop looking behind.

And honestly, the hockey wasn't that good in the "Original Six." Montreal got the rights to all the Quebec players. From 1945 to 1967 Montreal won the Cup nine times in 25 years beating out three other teams in the playoffs. Is it a big whoop? I mean really, take the nostalgia out of it for a second, is it really a big accomplishment? Hey, we won two series. Congratulations, here's the Stanley Cup. I mean, I'm sorry, it's just not a big deal. At least the Canadian Football League usually has eight teams, sometimes nine teams. To win a Grey Cup you need to win three games. Vancouver has six Lester Patrick Trophies, two PCHL Trophies, and four WHL titles between 1940 and 1970. So that's 12 championships compared to Montreal's nine. So what?

Look at the places hockey has been, professionally, in the western time zones and look at some of the names:

Vancouver Lions (yes before the CFL) Maroons, and Millionaires.
Calgary Stampeders (yes before the CFL) and Calgary Tigers
Edmonton Flyers (before Philadelphia Flyers) and Edmonton Eskimos (yes of CFL name)
Fresno Falcons
Hollywood Wolves
Los Angeles Monarchs (became the Kings)
New Westminster Royals (original capital of B.C.)
Oakland Oaks
Pasadena Panthers

Portland Eagles, Rosebuds, Penguins & Buckaroos (became Chicago Blackhawks)

San Diego Skyhawks

San Francisco Shamrocks (who could forget the Golden Seals? Became Cleveland Barons, then the Minnesota North Stars and then the Dallas Stars)

Saskatoon Quakers

Seattle Ironmen (also the Eskimos & Metropolitans & Stars)

Tacoma Rockets

Victoria Cougars (became Detroit Red Wings)

Denver, Colorado (Denver has had hockey dating back to 1901)

Want to talk about history? The Seattle Metropolitans were the first American team to win the Stanley Cup prior to any "Original Six" team and fundamentally changed the Stanley Cup rules which was only to be awarded in Canada. The PCHA created the ability for the NHL to use the Stanley Cup.

Again, there was no jet travel because it wasn't invented yet so the "Original Six" only denotes a period of time celebrating one of two professional hockey leagues prior to air travel. You could argue the talent wasn't as good in these leagues compared to the NHL. I agree. But there was a minor league operation, the AHL, operating in the east. There were several minor leagues playing in the United States in fact at the same time as the NHL.

Professional hockey players earned money in the PCHA then Western Hockey League and in those American minor leagues. And so they did in the Pacific Coast League. And since the PCL didn't play for the Stanley Cup since 1926 no one will ever know for sure how the talent levels actually stacked up between any of these leagues.

The western leagues could have challenged for the Stanley Cup but they never did. It's a costly venture to move teams by train, and for what purpose? There was none. They each had their own champions so who cared? (Incidentally in 1974 the Seattle Totems and Denver Spurs were granted NHL teams but it never came to fruition until the Colorado Rockies got a team in 1976, the Kansas City Scouts. Rockies is now the name of Denver's MLB team because the NHL didn't keep the name).

Was the talent in the NHL better than the other leagues in the 1960s? I think so. I think it's fair to say it was, however in a seven game series could you be confident an NHL team could beat any of the best teams in those other leagues? No. You can't be confident. And prior to the 1950s I think it was a toss up. And anyone who says the NHL was way better than the WHL are the same people that claimed the NHL players were waaaaaay better than the Russians. How'd that turn out in 1972?

Remember the PCHA did regularly win the Stanley Cup proving it was on par prior to World War Two. And if the Stanley Cup really was the end all to be all, why didn't the PCHL challenge it? I don't think they cared about the eastern NHL. I think there's a tendency to rewrite history as people get further from it. I think television made people think in the 1960s that the NHL was better than the WHL because television distorts like that. But I bet if the owners and mangers were alive today they'd tell you they weren't far behind the NHL and weren't concerned in the least. They probably were a bit annoyed with them claiming hockey supremacy when they didn't go past Chicago to play. It doesn't make sense. Here's an exclusively eastern time zone league claiming hockey supremacy. I think there probably was a collective shrug in western Canada and the United States. And besides, college football and MLB ruled supreme. Hockey was an afterthought in the US. And in B.C. lacrosse and horse racing were on par with hockey.

And the CFL ruled the west in the 1950s and 1960s in Canada.

As someone in the west who watches hockey in the west I can tell you there's dislike for the broadcast treatment of the western Canadian teams both from Bell and Rogers and prior to that the CBC. They use the "Original Six" garbage to no end. Sportsnet, the Rogers sports company which covers the NHL and owns some of the Leafs, closed its Vancouver bureau in favour of commenting about Vancouver games from Toronto, of all places. So the people commenting on Canucks games are indirectly affiliated with the Toronto Maple Leafs.

There's no pre or post game shows for viewers in Vancouver either. It's usually straight to Toronto Blue Jays MLB highlights after a Canucks game. Can you imagine watching a Los Angeles Kings game and after the game ESPN cuts away and goes to a post game show that's all about the New York Yankees? In your face Los Angeles! No, I don't think so.

NBC does the same thing featuring a large share of Chicago games and pushing the "Original Six" theme constantly on air (remember, Chicago is from Portland.) And then the NHL does it itself with Winter Classic games featuring "Original Six" matchups. Oh my God, does it ever end? Is there nobody in charge of the NHL marketing who realizes how distasteful this is in other markets? Then they sit there and wonder why the Arizona Coyotes are constantly in financial trouble. Well, I'm just throwing this out as a suggestion but perhaps it's not an "Original Six" team - in your face Arizona!! You suck and we say so. Every team except six teams are second class citizens and they suck.

What kind of marketing is this? Welcome to the NHL, some teams are way cooler than other teams, so suck it princess. Is it a good marketing strategy to offend 90 percent of the league's fans? I don't have a marketing degree but I can't imagine anyone would condone the practice in the marketing world. Here's a MacDonalds commercial featuring the original MacDonalds and all the rest of the MacDonalds are expansion teams and they suck. They're ok, but they're not as good as this original one in Des Plaines, Illinois. It's waaaay better than the one you go to so suck it! I don't think I've ever seen such a MacDonald's commercial.

The concentration of media coverage centered in Toronto is enormous. As a viewer, it's hard to figure out where the national broadcasts end and the Leafs start. Canada used to have a neutral third party called the Canadian Broadcast Corporation which would broadcast the games from coast-to-coast, and although it too faced issues with being Toronto centric, at least it had the appearance of neutrality as they were not connected to ownership of the Toronto Maple Leafs and they were funded by taxpayers nationwide and they had to answer to politicians.

I also understand Toronto drives a good portion of NHL revenue and so the media executives want to milk it as much as possible to pay off the $5.2 billion cost of the tv contract. And NHL teams throughout the league receive cheques for the national television contract. But a market like Vancouver, I believe, is already seeing the impact of Toronto centric on its fans who are staying away. Yes, I think it also has something to do with the product on the ice being terrible but it's also a heavy backlash against all things Toronto being force fed in the market and I know this because I can see it on twitter streams and hear it on the sports radio. For a team like Vancouver it's possibly going to lose millions of dollars in revenue in ticket sales and possibly lose franchise value as it was approaching the $1 billion market in value and has now dropped to $700 million in some estimates. How accurate the estimates are I don't know but it's probably concerning to quite a few NHL franchises.

But I do know the Canucks created the Sunday night game as a way of getting away from the Saturday

Toronto Maple Leafs game and to get their own media attention. When Sportsnet got the television rights the Canucks lost their exclusive Sunday night game which had boosted their team's franchise value and Sportsnet began showing, you guessed it, Toronto Maple Leafs on Sunday night (along with the other Canadian teams.) It's quite possible Rogers made the bid for the national tv contract in part because they could see the sky rocketing Canuck franchise value.

According to statista.com, the statistics portal, NHL revenue in 2005/06 season was $2.3 billion and in 2015/16 it was $4.1 billion. But it was also just under $4 billion for 2014/15 season possibly indicating revenue has plateaued. Some of this may be linked to the entertainment value associated with the NHL. In other words other people may be turning it off. It's possible there isn't as many of the younger generations watching hockey or buying tickets as there used to be and so you could see a drop off; and you would see this drop off in other sports as well. The NBA revenues went from $3.3 billion in 2005 to $5.87 billion in 2015 and is estimated to be at $8.3 billion in 2016 because of a new TV contract with ESPN. However, ESPN lost nine million viewers from 2008 to 2017. The sports market may be getting tougher with fewer cable viewers and more digital products competing for eyeballs and ESPN faced massive layoffs across their platforms recently and it impacted their NHL coverage to say the least.

And from a business point of view Vancouver was the fourth highest revenue producing NHL team ahead of Boston, Detroit and Chicago. And so I wonder if the NHL had focused more on the other teams instead of just six teams if they wouldn't have arrived at a better destination financially than they are now.

I think it's fair to say the sports market is getting tougher because of saturation. It's harder to get your voice heard today than 40 years ago. And so why is the NHL on-air product so stale compared to the NFL? The face of hockey in the U.S. is Doc Emrick and Darren Pang and Pierre McGuire. Okay, they may be good at their jobs, they may not be. It's in the eye of the beholder. I personally think they're God awful. But just take a second to look at them. They're short, bald guys, with high-pitched voices. It's not screaming sports at you. Where are the former NHL athletes doing the broadcasts? The play-by-play and the colour? Emrick was a baseball guy and in my opinion it shows. If you look at NBC ratings in the U.S. they're not great. The 2012 Cup Finals were on pace to be the lowest ratings on record. There's been some decent increases too to be fair. But it's not like it's a steady increase. And yet, they're still there, the same group of guys.

I keep hearing the same thing - Americans just aren't used to the game yet - to which I would reply, Americans have had NHL hockey for over a century. As I said previously, Los Angeles has had professional hockey since World War II. Do you think someone might clue in it could be a dislike of the broadcasters on air? Maybe the ratings are linked to really bad looking and sounding people? Now again, they have their fans too. I'm just not one of them. But obviously lots of people like them as well. But don't you just change things just as a matter of fact to see if you get ratings boosts? Don't you go ahead and cross that bridge? The NFL certainly isn't shy about changing things up if it's not getting the ratings they want.

Would I watch an NBC broadcast if Mario Lemieux was the colour commentator? Uhh, do you think? Where's Gretzky on the broadcasts? Mark Messier? How about Guy Lafleur? What about Marcel Dionne? NHL stars play the game and just vanish into thin air like puffs from a vapour cigarette.

The point is the relationship we build as fans with the NHL players isn't continued after they retire. In the NFL you can continue hearing from your heroes every Sunday. They don't really retire too far. They're still there for us and our beer and chips as we fall asleep on the couch. The NFL just hired ex-Dallas Cowboy Tony Romo. He didn't go too far. From the field to the booth. It's comforting. But NHL stars just blow up like the drummer in Spinal Tap. Now these hockey stars may be asked to take broadcasting jobs and just don't want them. But I'm guessing if you threw $2 million per year on a five year contract for Wayne Gretzky to do colour on NBC hockey games on Saturday he would show up for work. They're athletes. Show them the money! as Tom Cruise says to Cuba Gooding Jr. in the movie Jerry Maguire. Back up the Brinks truck and get some of these stars back in front of the camera. And get them to loosen up and let us into their worlds. Stars drive ratings. Keep them around.

In the NHL on NBC we get failed GMs and bald assistants ad nauseam. I'm sorry, but quite frankly, you're not interesting. I never knew you and I never cared about your careers. I didn't have a playing card for a GM with his drafts and trades on it or fourth liners. The script of how it's done is there for the NHL because the NFL wrote it. Do what they do. Get the retiring hot stars, pop them in the booth. And get the guys with deep voices and hair calling the games. Don't mind with the sopranos. Get the baritones. Look good. Sound good.

And as for media in Canada well it's the same story. Where's the stars? Where's the pipes? Jim Hughson for Sportsnet who calls the games is really good but he's all alone and all he does are Toronto games and his sidekick is about as interesting as stale milk. Bob Cole was good but Harry Neale was better. So was Howie Meeker. Again, the framework of what should happen has been set in Canada - Cole and Neale. (And yes I get Neale was a retired GM which I just said weaw not interesting. Neale was.) Hughson and Brian Burke would be delightful. Brian Burke, now the President of the Calgary Flames is an absolute gold mine and media darling. What's he doing in Calgary? He should be on

Saturday night in Canada or anchoring NBC. And John Davidson who is now President of the Columbus Blue Jackets was also spectacular as a broadcaster. Davidson is badly missed on NBC broadcasts and he and Burke need to be there, front and centre boosting ratings along with Gretzky, Lemieux, and Brett Hull.

So there are stars in the game but they just don't get the centre stage and I wonder if it's the money. Oh, I forgot, Mike Milbury is on NBC. Ok, I didn't forget but he's just so forgettable and unoriginal. I think he's copying Don Cherry but I'm not sure. And Don Cherry invented broadcasting in Canada but where's his replacement? There's no one in the pipeline. But then again since no one can replace Cherry shouldn't they start looking for someone with their own schtick? Maybe Georges Laraque might be a good start. He's pretty outspoken and heavily involved in hockey and the camera loves him and he's bilingual and interesting. As long as he avoids the temptation of being Don Cherry and just is himself I think he might bring some pretty good television to hockey broadcasts. Another possibility is Florida goalie Roberto Luongo. He is an absolute must if they can coax him onto the broadcasts after his retirement and just let him be himself. He's extremely sharp witted, funny and the camera loves him, and he loves the camera and he's French-Canadian.

The most important thing about diversifying the media is getting out of Toronto. The number one requirement of all national broadcasts moving forward needs to be "anything but from Toronto area." Toronto has to be cut off and shut off in order for the NHL to move forward as a league. It's so ridiculously boring and predictable.

SALARY CAP

The salary cap was intended to level the playing field so teams didn't have $30 million difference in salary such as 1994. They wanted to level the playing field and make small market teams viable. In theory it's a good idea and the NHL should be applauded for trying to help small market teams. The Toronto Maple Leafs lead the NHL in committed salary at $79 million (cap maximum) while the Arizona Coyotes are at the basement at $56 million for this season (cap minimum is $55 million.) Revenue sharing allows Arizona and Florida to remain afloat.

But what happens is GMs/owners eventually decide they can't lose their free agent players because they're in such short supply and they end up at the salary ceiling instead of the salary floor as intended with the salary cap. So some small market teams overspend to compete.

And as is the case with any business deal, it can have grey areas. Large revenue teams may try to circumvent the hard cap. A team like the Leafs, hypothetically for example, could find faults in an older non-useful player resulting from his physical in training camp and management could decide small problems which might be overlooked if they wanted the player would now be enough to fail such a player so they could pay them not to play. It's a grey area. One such Leafs player Joffrey Lupul made this allegation in September of 2017 but quickly deleted his allegations and later apologized. Lupul had sports hernia surgery in 2015/16 season and hasn't played since. The Leafs delete his $5.2 million salary from their salary cap each year and Lupul doesn't have to play in the AHL to get his money because he failed his physical. This is fortunate for the Leafs because they can put him on injury reserve and not need to use a contract on him. It's referred to as "Robidas Island" named after Stephane Robidas who was put on injury reserve for two years by the Leafs because of knee problems. He then got a job with the Leafs management. It's not contrary to the CBA to put players on injured reserve and leave them there. But teams with smaller revenues couldn't afford such a large "Robidas Island" of players being paid not to play. And in fairness Robidas said he couldn't play.

Other ways to cut costs, whether you wanted to be at the maximum or the minimum, is to eliminate the journeyman. There's enormous benefit in the salary cap era for a team to dress 18-year-olds right out of the draft or as soon as possible because they're cheap. And the 29-year-old established player is squeezed out of the NHL. There's no room for the middle players. There's young kids and established stars.

And as I've laid out the argument in previous pages as to why hockey sucks it doesn't get any better than the one sentence: There's young kids and established stars. And there isn't enough of either to go around. In order for great players to be great they need great help. You can't just put a Wayne Gretzky on the ice and expect him to win alone. He never did without help. He took a pretty good Los Angeles team to the Finals once but no Stanley Cup. A really good example is the 2011 (I know, I know, another Vancouver reference) Vancouver Canucks when they lost their two best veteran blue liners Dan Hamhuis and Aaron Rome they found themselves icing a raw rookie in Chris Tanev straight out of college because they had bumped right up to the salary cap. If they'd had another veteran ready to go they would have won the Cup. And so injuries play a massive role in winning in the salary cap era. Not necessarily because of their team's salary because you get salary relief when they're put on longterm injury reserve but because there's no one available to sign or to acquire via trade and you end up icing raw rookies.

Salary caps prevent trades. Trades were the best part of hockey for fans, especially young fans. GMs were able to horse trade their way out of a losing slump or a bad season if they were good. Nowadays I don't even know why teams have GMs. They don't make trades anymore. It's a rare thing. You might get a few trades in the summer when teams have salary cap flexibility (they can go over the cap by 10 percent) but very few once the puck drops in October. Part of being a fan is the excitement of hearing trade rumours on the radio or reading about it in the newspaper or online. Your team, other teams, it doesn't matter. It creates interest for the game. It gets a buzz going. But now with "No Movement Clauses" and "No Trade Clauses" added to contracts to entice players to sign or re-sign with a team you run out of players to trade, even if teams had salary cap room.

Salary caps pressure players to accept less money in contracts to allow teams to "build a team" to win. Everyone in the league is a private contractor and should be concerned with how much money they can make for themselves. If a player dares to make the maximum allowed under the salary cap they are often deemed as selfish which is ridiculous. And no one has claimed the maximum amount of allowable salary under the salary cap era. A team like the Edmonton Oilers should be riddled with salary cap issues as a reward for taking first overall pick after first overall pick but they signed for less than maximum money.

There should be more players available on free agency but there isn't. Teams sign up all their free agents before July 1st (the first day everyone can sign unrestricted free agents) so they can't be signed by other teams. So there are two days in the NHL season which should offer a great deal of excitement - free agency day and trade deadline day. Unfortunately fans only get warm milk. The teams are all still in the playoff hunt on trade deadline day so there is a shortage of available players. And on free agency day players on a good team are pressured to stay there and have already re-signed. And so you can get teams staying at the bottom of the ranking for years with no change because there are no free agents available to sign or trades to make. Even if you could find a trade, most players have a no trade clause.

What should happen is signing of restricted free agents with less penalty. Bad teams should be able to prey on teams bumping into the salary cap. But you almost never see teams signing other teams restricted free agents. The Edmonton Oilers are a good example. They have signed Connor McDavid to almost the maximum available money and had a restricted free agent in Leon Draisatl who was better than McDavid in the playoffs. He was available to all the teams in the NHL for the signing. Other teams could have forced the Oilers to a salary cap issue by signing Draisatl to a maximum cap deal for eight years; however teams were reluctant to do it because it would cost four first round picks and more importantly other teams would then treat them like a pariah.

So if you can't draft a player and you can't sign a free agent or a restricted free agent and you can't trade because of the salary cap and no movement clauses - what's the point of following the sport? If you follow a bad team they're going to be a bad team unless they fluke out in the draft lottery. So basically you're sitting around waiting for lady luck because there's nothing else that can be done. Nice.

I think we can all understand the NHL, like other leagues, wants parity. It wants every team to have a chance. But in order to do this you must be able to let teams get what they need quickly. You can't have teams languishing for 10 years or more at the bottom of the standings. The Winnipeg Jets are a prime example of this. They were terrible in Atlanta and had to move to Winnipeg where they've been equally as horrific. If you're going to have a salary cap then you have to force player movement. You have to ban no movement clauses and no trade clauses. And you have to cap the maximum amount of years on contracts at four and you have to make them non-guaranteed so teams can cut bad contracts. More talent must be on the move in the NHL.

SCHEDULE

Would there be anything wrong with playing every team once home and away? The top 16 teams would get in at the end of it no matter where they were from. The bottom half would not. Top seed would get bottom seed throughout the playoffs. It would be a reward for finishing first overall in the NHL. Maybe even give them a first week bye or choose their opponent. I guess the simple answer is yes, the NHL would only have 62 games. But wouldn't that be great? A first round matchup of Toronto and Los Angeles. Imagine the joy of Toronto management having to travel outside their time zone.

But no we don't get a real simple version of the schedule in the NHL. We get 31 teams with uneven conferences and uneven schedules. The uneven schedules meaning different numbers of teams in divisions and inter-division play and conference play and different levels of travel. What happens is an unbalanced travel schedule advantage for the eastern teams. So you would think there would be financial compensation from east to west to make up for this. But no, the western teams don't get to have extra players or extra salary cap to make it even which would be the logical step. Does it make any sense at all to have one league with different amounts of difficulty? It's obviously a more difficult feat for the west than the east to win a Stanley Cup as well because of the same lack of travel in the east. And the 82 games is a reach for a physical sport to expect a good game every night. Too often a dud of a game is served up.

As I previously mentioned, there's too much of a difference between playoff and regular season play. I hear all the time, "Oh playoff hockey is so great." So what does it say about the 82 games previous? They weren't trying? I'm sure they were trying but not giving the 100% effort. They weren't selling out every night. And as fans, how did it become acceptable? Everyone goes to a regular season game knowing there's not really a full effort because we can compare it to the playoffs in the first round and see a massive jump in intensity. It doesn't compare to the NFL where the games are all playoff meaningful. The intensity is almost the same from game one to the Super Bowl.

The NHL schedule is changed every few years so it's hard for fans to keep up with. The lack of consistency costs fan interest. I still want to see Minnesota, Toronto, Detroit. St. Louis and Chicago in the Norris Division like it was from 1982-1992.

Then there's the labour disruptions every time they get to the end of the CBA. Then after the schedule disruption, sometimes costing an entire season, there's new rules, a new schedule and more expansion. This current contract ends in 2020 but notice to leave the contract can be given in 2019 for the following year. So given the track record of the NHL and its players being unable to come to agreements, fans can expect labour disruptions in two years. Players right now are signing with more money up front so they won't be as badly affected by the coming league shutdown. So it tells fans it's going to be bad. They're planning for it. So at most as a fan you get eight years of hockey in a row. Then once the year is scrubbed because there's no contract agreement the draft order is messed up and rebuilding teams get the middle finger again and teams going for the Stanley Cup miss their windows. It kills league momentum.

And then every four years they stop the NHL in the middle of the schedule for the Olympics to play the most awful scrub hockey on large ice surfaces if the Olympics are in Europe or Asia and NHL sizes if its in North America. It doesn't make any sense. And the hockey is terrible. A lot of Canadian media likes to sell it as good hockey but it's garbage. I hear all the time where people were when Sidney Crosby scored a goal to win Canada an Olympic gold in a tournament with eight teams in the competition. Realistically Canada was one of four teams that could win the gold. So was it really a big whoop? I was dirt biking on a mountain and someone in a 4 by 4 truck stopped beside me and said, "Canada won the gold!" To which I replied to her: "In what?" She looked at me and said "Crosby scored a goal in OT." I said: "Oh, who was Canada playing?" She replied: "The United States." And I said, "Oh, that sucks for Ryan Kesler (then a Canuck) but I guess it's good for Luongo." I mean really, who do you cheer for? I like Americans. I wasn't interested in cheering against them. It would be better for the NHL if they had won.

It's a pointless tournament held every four years at the wrong time of the year that disheartens the nation when its a reminder how thin the world talent pool is. As I said before if you did Olympic ball hockey now I'm paying attention because you can have South American teams, African teams, European teams, Asian teams, Indian teams - the whole world can participate. I'd love to see ball hockey in the summer Olympics. A ball hockey gold medal would be worth something. But can you really brag about winning a ice hockey gold medal where only four teams have a chance to win? The USA, Canada, Russia and Sweden can win. I guess you could add Finland but it's a bit of a long shot. Then again Russia hasn't won it in years so maybe Finland over

Russia. But the point is there's almost no one playing the game. I'm not sure anyone in India is marveling at Canada for winning a gold medal in hockey. I think their answer might be: "Duh?" If China, India, South America and Africa aren't participating in the sport, is it really a worldwide sport?

And is the Olympic hockey really that good? Does anyone need to see Canada beat Norway 11-0 every time? The only thing the tournament does is torture real hockey fans watching France play Norway or something waiting for the NHL to restart. The teams are thrown together and play a few games then if they win four games they win a gold.

The stars struggle. Crosby had a terrible Olympics in 2010 so did Ovechkin. It's a ridiculous tournament for ice hockey to be involved in. Fortunately, the NHL has said they are not going to South Korea. Thank goodness because who would stop their league for three weeks so their fans can watch games at 3 am? It's ridiculous. I mean you have to be a hardcore hockey nutbar to have watched the live games in the Russian Olympics.

And then there's the Olympics themselves. Why are professionals going to what is supposed to be an amateur athlete event? When did it become ok to send professionals? It used to be a big deal for a lot of amateur hockey athletes to get together and train for a few months and go and represent their country and get on television maybe for the only time in their lives. For example the USA at Lake Placid and "Do you believe in miracles?" Sending professionals isn't the same. I didn't watch the gold medal game in Vancouver between the USA and Canada in 2010 because it was 15 degrees celsius out and sunny in winter and I couldn't care less about whether some guy making $10 million beat another guy making $10 million for a gold medal. And I wasn't alone in not caring. Was there any doubt Canada would win it? And if they didn't win it, would we care? I found it to be petty, ugly and unimaginative. I loved the amateurs in the game. To me, amateurs are what the Olympics are all about. It's about cinderella stories. It's about people working their tails off for their one shot and seeing them get it. Dreams are fantastic to watch on television. A bunch of professionals pummeling a small country isn't fun to watch.

And are the Olympics really a vessel of virtue? It's pretty corrupt isn't it? And then there's drugs involved in it. Russia's been kicked out for cheating, again. What else is new?

And there's the injuries. The schedule is compressed to make the three week break possible so you can squeeze in the Olympics. In the past five Olympics the eastern conference has won the Stanley Cup in four of those five olympic years with Los Angeles in 2014 the only team to break the pattern. Teams like the New York Islanders lost their star John Tavares at the Olympics. In a previous Olympics in Italy the Canucks lost two defenseman and missed the playoffs as did the Islanders in 2014 when they lost Tavares. Teams sending more players to the Olympics than others can also be at a disadvantage when it comes to making the playoffs as their stars will have more mileage on them during the season. So what's the point of fan investment in the NHL during an Olympic year if they're going?

Wait until Toronto Maple Leafs centre Auston Matthews goes to an Olympics to play for the USA and gets injured by some guy from Switzerland who's trying to make a name for himself. Then you'll see "national" media finally realize the Olympics are a mistake. Then all of a sudden there will be mass hysteria about getting professionals out of the Olympics.

As for the regular season NHL schedule there needs to be an attempt to even out the travel burdens. The east has to travel more and the west less. A North South conference setup might create this balance. Separate the New York and Toronto area teams into different conferences completely. Align divisions to correct travel.

For example, in the NFL, the NY Giants, Dallas Cowboys and Washington Redskins are in the same division. Get away from the East West concept and get into National Hockey Conference and American Hockey Conference.

Schedule back-to-back games in the same city to create some intrigue and perhaps rivalries and cut travel. The season needs to start in September not October. It should start on Labour Day when the kids go back to school. It's a natural order of things. And playoffs need to start in April and be wrapped up at the end of May. It can't go into June or July. Summer hockey has to stop. It's up against the NBA and it needs its own time slot. What they're doing right now isn't helping US television ratings very much. Try something drastic. At the end of March, wrap the season up.

PERSONALITY

Think of all the guys who provide entertainment in the NHL like a Charles Barkley did in the NBA. It's a short list, isn't it? It's hard to find a personality in the game today but the NHL used to have at least one on every team like a Dave "Tiger" Williams. Hockey had personalities. But they disappeared. The hockey culture is almost military in nature with everyone conforming and those who don't are shipped out. One of the reasons is the NHL lost its tough guys who were almost always the entertainers. Tiger Williams, Tie Domi and Dave The Hammer Schultz are just a few of the notorious brawlers the NHL lost and when they left and weren't replaced, the personality in hockey left too.

It's almost like the NHL culture prevents personality today. Nashville Predator's P.K. Subban is a bit of an entertainer. During the 2017 NHL playoff Finals Subban suggested Sidney Crosby had bad breath. It was outstanding entertainment including the fight with Crosby on the ice. It was highly enjoyable and the highlight of the Finals. And he was roundly criticized for providing enjoyment. Ryan Kesler of the Anaheim Ducks is another entertainer who gets the selling tickets part of the game but who is always roundly attacked by the media.

Wanting the spotlight isn't part of hockey culture and it needs to change. Every team needs an entertainer or a heel. It's the whole purpose of the game. But too often you get drones on the ice who don't let their personalities shine through because I think the culture of the locker room is to be team first even on the ice. And when they do provide entertainment the media is the first to lash out at them for being a "me" player and not a "team" player. Where's the GMs to defend the player? Where's the rest of the players stepping forward on his behalf to say "we love it!" "Keep going!"

Coaches are too bland today. John Tortorella is the biggest entertainer behind the bench today but 30 years ago he was common place. Now he's unique in the NHL. Tortorella was fired in Vancouver mainly for getting into a fight in the corridor behind the benches with Calgary Flames coach Bob Hartley. It was spectacular theatre. And the games afterwards were as interesting as they could be between two struggling teams. Fans don't get enough of this type of entertainment. It's a show, it's theatre and Tortorella is one of the few people in the NHL who gets it and he got fired, several times, even though he won a Stanley Cup and his teams are usually over-performing.

Goal celebrations are no longer unique. When a player scores a goal he skates to the bench and high-fives them as he skates past. It's a junior hockey move which got into the NHL and it needs to leave. Guys used to score a goal and tap shinpads and head to the faceoff circle at centre ice and twirl around or lean on their sticks or nod to the crowd. Everyone had just a little bit different way of showing off after a goal. It was for the crowd and not for the guys on the bench. After Gretzky scored a goal the camera would zoom in on him, the spotlights would shine on him and you could see him smiling at Kurri and they would be talking back and forth. It was interesting. Players need to stop running to the bench but go to centre ice and take a bow or wave or nod or finger the crowd. It's part of the entertainment package.

Speaking of Gretzky, what about the silver stick and the shirt tucked on one side into his pants? It was entertaining. Why didn't the NHL follow up on it? Where's the golden sticks? The bright blues or neon greens? Today you have Ovechkin with his orange skate laces but he's the only one that seems to say to the fans look at me, watch me. He got criticized by the media for "lighting his stick on fire" after his 50th goal. It was a big deal and it was fantastic entertainment and a little throwback to Jimi Hendrix burning his guitar. Who can forget Tiger Williams riding his stick to centre ice and windmilling his right arm at the same time? Outstanding entertainment. No one complained about Tiger doing it. He was selling the game. It's good for the game and good for the game means more revenue and more money in player's pockets. It doesn't mean stop being really nice to fans and media it just means be a hot dog. Sell it a bit.

Where's the hockey brawls? They're a thing of the past. And it's a shame. Fighting provided an entertainment value but I think what it really did was show the fans they were trying and the crest on the sweater meant something. They cared about each other and the sweater. It forged a bond between the fan and the sweater. Fans knew they cared enough to fight for the sweater and the city and so they bonded with them. It's disappeared. There's more brawls in baseball than hockey today. It's a part of the game fans miss.

The NHL is a Shakespeare play or should be. Shakespeare wrote for the mob, not the well-to-do. It was the commoners he spoke to and the NHL used to be for the mob as well. But it's become too serious, the players and coaches are too stoic. Take a page from wrestling's playbook and teach these NHL players about entertainment and to embrace their character on the ice. They need to encourage colour in the game in the uniforms, the sticks, the laces. Individuals sell the game not common drones. There should be 20 types of helmets based not just on safety but on individualizing. Some of the players should wear tattered old uniforms, some should be brand new. The whole goal of a GM should be to introduce individualism to a team and helping players find their show business.

It's amazing to me that you could be in the "entertainment" business and not have anybody on any team in any management capacity (that I know of) who is from the entertainment industry. You would think the first person you would hire in the entertainment business is someone who has entertainment experience. Yes, everyone should play hockey at a very high level. But what about selling tickets? Selling eyeballs on televisions? The Canucks had a guy at their tryout camp a decade ago named Pecker. I'm sorry, even if he's not as good a player as someone else doesn't the name on the jersey get him into the lineup? "Pecker scores!" It was sitting there on a silver platter for the team.

Come hell or high water the NHL has to bust out of the drone business. It's the same team playing the same team wearing the same colours each night with the same score. Yes dedicated fans will always follow their teams. But it's not growing the game. It isn't expanding the base. I've touched on just a few possibilities but the main goal of every team is to get each of these players looking different and acting differently.

NHL teams have coaches for defense, coaches for goalies, even a few offense coaches, media coaches, video coaches but what they don't have are entertainment coaches. Hockey is a unique opportunity for the entertainment business. Things exist in hockey such as being sent to the penalty box... all by yourself... with the camera all over you and just you. It doesn't happen in any other sport (except lacrosse). It has faceoffs highlighting two individuals and it's unique. Coaches are on benches behind the team and that's unique. Teams are sitting behind boards leaning over them and that's unique. Hockey and only hockey has a captain and assistant captains and that's unique. You see other leagues try to copy hockey with their fake "Cs" on the uniform. Hockey is screaming entertainment but it's shuttered right now. Hopefully the NHL can start realizing it has the best opportunity for growth out of any sport if it embraces goals and individualism. If the NHL can turn the page on the "defense" and make every possible stride to provide entertainment each night it will surpass everything. The possibilities are only limited by imagination.

SUMMARY

Getting the game out of the doldrums needs to start with cleaning the game up in Canada. Goals and only goals need to start mattering. And the best way to get this done is with fundamentally altering the way we coach kids. We need to stop coaching kids. Hockey can't be coached. You can teach some basics. You can teach some power skating. But the rest of the game has to be kids getting to 10,000 hours.

And every time you get on the ice and you stop kids and tell them to do this drill or stand here the clock stops. They'll never get to 10,000 hours with coaches in the way. There needs to be way fewer games and way less dependency on rep teams. In fact the whole concept of this process needs to be changed. The key thing for everyone to remember is the 10,000 hours. If kids get it playing ball hockey and ice hockey then fine. Scrimmages and free play matter more than drills. Drills stop the process of learning. Scrimmages are where they learn in actual situations.

Less is more in coaching. And less is more in goaltending equipment. It's time to really evaluate the size of the goaltending pads and to work with companies to create form-fitting gear. The whole concept of hockey has to be turned into entertainment. The speed has to be removed and the hockey put back in. I want to see what people can do with the puck and the stick. I couldn't care less about how fast someone can skate. It really doesn't float my boat or anyone else's boat. How fast can you turn? How quickly can you stop? How quickly can you stick handle? Those things matter. The slap shot matters. The wrist and snap shots matter.

Get the blue lines and red lines back in the game. Slow it down and get the hockey back. It's not a track meet.

SOLUTIONS

LABOUR DAY WEEKEND START
Start the NHL season on Labour Day and end it in March/April. Get the playoffs finished in May.

SPEED
Get the speed out of the game. I know that sounds counter-intuitive to progress but in hockey speed does some very bad things. First off, skating is fast - period. There's no need to make it faster than it already is normally. But what speed does in hockey is cause serious injuries. And secondly speed kills offense in hockey. The puck always can travel faster than anyone can skate. A pass can be 60 mph. Put the rules back pre-1999.

TWENTY-YEAR-OLD DRAFT
First and foremost it lets parents be parents with their kids even if hockey is included. It removes the pressure of making the cut at 13 and instead bumps it to 15 at a minimum. It lets all the leagues above peewee improve. It returns the love of the game to the kids.

It's safer because kids don't have to leave home when they're barely teenagers putting them at risk of a Graham James, sex predator.

It improves the product because teams select players they know more about. Rebuilding teams will actually get immediate help with their first round draft picks right through the entire first round.

Thirdly with increased experience and certainty it improves the talent at the NHL level by getting more players able to compete on the ice.

Lastly and most importantly - it puts the National Collegiate Athletic Association into play for all these children. It's the most important thing for all these kids considering hockey as a career. What if it doesn't work? It doesn't work for 99.99% of these kids and parents. So then what? Where do they go then? Junior hockey in Canada has started a program to help pay for school after their junior careers which is good. However, at their age when they would enter college these kids are out of step with the rest of their high-school graduation class who went to college or university at 18. When you're on a school roll - you can't ever stop. You need to keep going and finish. The NCAA would become an even better option for these kids.

Canadian universities could then apply to become part of the NCAA hockey program and become a viable alternative right along with the American colleges. And colleges in Canada could run a competing program with high-level hockey and college programs as an extra alternative for kids who don't want to go to university but may want a technical diploma from a college like a British Columbia Institute of Technology.

All of these kids would get two years of education and be eligible for NHL drafts; many of them, with the support of their NHL club, may wish them to complete a full degree while continuing to improve their athletic abilities and then jump to the NHL at 22 or 23. And for those kids wanting a doctorate they could be in the NHL at 25 with seven years of education in their back-pocket.

It's so important these kids proceed through high school with their friends with the understanding academic achievement is first and foremost and no decision on a hockey career need take place before the age of 18. This will also open the door for late-bloomers.

REMOVAL OF REP TEAMS

No rep teams before the age of 13. Parents need to be backed right off of the "hockey careers" mentality which starts with kids skating full-time at two. Removing Rep Teams enforces the point that their child won't play in the NHL and that's just about a guarantee. The same percentage of children starting ice hockey at 10 make the NHL as those starting at five. And it's still a certainty they won't play in the NHL whether they start rep at seven or 13.

There's no need for kids to even play ice hockey before the age of 10. Skating and hockey are two separate sports and the emphasis on hockey must be returned. There are so many hockey stars who didn't even start skating before the age of 10 or playing ice hockey until they were in their teens. There is no correlation between starting ice hockey early and making the NHL. It is almost completely random and dependent on genetics and chance. Power skating can be learned in a four week summer class when the child is ready especially in their mid-teens where they will adapt what they need for themselves.

RENAMING LEAGUES FROM HOUSE AND REPRESENTATIVE TO HOCKEY DEVELOPMENT & SKATING DEVELOPMENT LEAGUES

Kids leave hockey at 13 in droves because house league is considered inferior to representative so why bother proceeding when it's considered lame and they've missed the cut for the NHL? Wrong, wrong and wrong. The conversation must be turned from this mindset as not everyone can afford representative or wants to be in a pressure league.

There is a good solution if you get your mind off of the ice.

Rename House to Hockey Development and combine the ice sessions with ball hockey sessions. This stresses it's a development league for kids who want to be really good at hockey. This drastically cuts costs AND improves hockey players.

Renaming Representative to Skating Development makes it clear this program offers more skating development but also more expense and more rules.

Don't make kids choose at 13. Take the choice away. Take it away from parents too. You have two options. One league focuses on skating. One league focuses on hockey development. And there's no reason in the hockey league you couldn't introduce lacrosse to them from time to time. It's only limited by imagination.

There are two separate avenues to the NHL and both give children a 99.99% chance of not making the NHL. Clearly explain to children with handouts the avenues available to making the NHL INCLUDING using the Hockey or Skating avenue. Show them clearly they only need to tryout for a Junior A, Tier II team at 17 or 18 and to show them the NCAA schools offering hockey programs and hockey tryouts. Show them it can start at 18 not end at 13. Work with the NCAA and work with the Junior A, Tier II teams to flood the Independent leagues with literature talking about their schools.

DEVELOPMENT PROGRAM LAW

Regulations from the government of Canada and US governments limiting "pro-development" of hockey players under the age of 18. You can't have parents feeling pressure to spend $50,000 on top of rep league fees to "develop" their child into a pro-hockey player. Make minimum ages of 16 for attending development camps and a maximum cap under the age of 18 at $5,000 per year per child. Over the age of 18 people can go nuts. The US and Canada are free countries. This should facilitate development of the same coaching and refereeing schools at colleges offering these hockey programs. You might even see some colleges offering hockey instruction on top of sponsoring their hockey team which could qualify for student loans. It wouldn't mean less business for development schools - it would mean more development with better effects. And there needs to be an elimination of parents chasing parents down the development road with buckets of cash.

GOALTENDER EQUIPMENT

Goalie gear has to shrink. If forwards can block pucks without goalie gear then why do goalies need so much protection?

The goalie pads must stop above the knees.

The goalie pads must have irregular sides so when laid flat they expose ice surface.

Skinnier pads.

Shorter pads.

The glove and blockers must shrink a further 25 percent and the goaltender stick 10 percent.

The pants and the shirts must be skin tight. And it has to be inspected by the referee in front of the crowds like the referee inspects boxing gloves before a boxing match.

The entertainment value of the goalie must come back and these changes should allow more goals while bringing back real reflex goalies.

NETS BACK TO THE BOARDS

The thought was to make more room behind the net to make plays by moving the net forward but all it did was make more room for the defensemen to make plays. Good forwards can take advantage of the original small area.

BLUE LINES MOVED BACK

Making the neutral zone smaller decreased the area for skilled forwards to go to work and made it further from the blue line to the net after they've made their offensive move which is a defender's advantage. It's also made it easier for people to institute defensive postures.

RETURN THE RED LINE

Removing the red line was supposed to increase scoring - it hasn't. It's turned the game into a "speed skating" drill and nothing could be worse for entertainment value. On top of that teams have figured out how to run a Trap system in it.

BALANCED SCHEDULE

Do more to ensure eastern teams travel as much as the western teams. It has to be balanced. A good start would be a Northern and Southern Conference and to ensure teams in the east get out of their time zones often.

Financial compensation for west to make up for travel imbalance. Western teams get to have extra players or extra salary cap to make it even.

Seasons need to start in September not October and the Stanley Cup must be handed out in May.

TORONTO DEFLATION

There's way too much Toronto in the NHL. Yes, they have a head office in New York but since Rogers bought the TV rights to the NHL it's more important than ever to remove all head office associations with Toronto to the west to balance out New York. Los Angeles would be the preferred location. There must be a good deal of distance between the broadcast rights holder and any NHL offices. The perception is it's too easy for Rogers to influence the NHL if they're right next door. They should be kept at arms length. And there should be an independent ombudsman appointed between the editorial staff at Rogers Sportsnet in Canada and Rogers ownership which also owns some of the Toronto Maple Leafs.

The ombudsman used to be a part of the Canadian Broadcast Corporation which held the TV rights in Canada before Rogers bought it. This public involvement kept the broadcaster at arm's length from the teams. I don't want the aspersion held Rogers is doing anything untoward. I'm sure they are not. I'm sure the NHL is perfectly aware of this perception and has taken steps to keep the two entities separate. And after Rogers paid $5.2 billion for TV rights it should expect the value of its team, the Toronto Maple Leafs, to increase.

The goal is to keep mindful of the other 30 teams in the NHL and especially the other Canadian markets whose fans often feel slighted by Toronto. And let's face it, the Toronto market, and it's media, is disliked by the rest of Canada almost uniformly. The ombudsman is there to keep it balanced and to make sure the NHL isn't just broadcast and promotion exclusively of the Toronto Maple Leafs by Toronto media who also work for the same company as the team. It's a difficult situation but it is workable.

SALARY CAP

The NFL salary cap works because of the availability of talent. And at $167 million per team it has the GDP of some small countries. And it has no guaranteed salaries. The NHL at $75 million per team ties talented players up almost indefinitely because they're such a valuable commodity. Not that NFL quarterbacks aren't a valuable commodity, but there are at least three franchise quarterbacks per NFL draft.

The NHL has an elite talent every decade. So in order to balance this out between those with franchise players and those without franchise players there must be a lower cap number, and a smaller contract in years.

In the NHL franchise players must be designated and maximum contract years must be set at four years. The NHL has a problem where only teams with these franchise players usually win a Stanley Cup. A Connor McDavid or an Auston Matthews, for example, must be limited to four years in Edmonton or Toronto and seen as an NHL commodity, not a team commodity. They must hit the open market several times during their careers and the current team must be limited on what they can bid to keep him and penalized with draft picks if he signs for a lower than maximum cap salary. The goal is to maximize these rare commodities especially in large US markets.

No movement and no trade clauses must be banned to encourage trades.

In other words there must be more than one way to win a Stanley Cup other than winning a lottery every 10 years. The desperate need for a franchise player must be eliminated so teams only need several top 10 picks to be competitive again. It may be adjusted once the talent source problems are corrected.

Extra salary cap room for teams based on travel.

Independent doctors must do team physicals to prevent teams from deliberately failing players at physicals so they can bury contracts they don't like on injured reserve.

ONE REFEREE
Two referees are in the way and they make the same bad calls as the one referee.

PLAYER SAFETY & REFEREE MANAGEMENT TO A NEUTRAL PARTY
Obviously moving the NHL back to one referee is a good start. Names on the back of the jersey are a good second. But the entire player safety department (that levies suspensions) must be removed from the hands of the NHL and the guidelines of the general managers and

into a neutral third party that no NHL executive can ever talk with.

And the supervision of the referees must also be moved to the same third party. Referees should never be in direct contact with the NHL. If they communicate it should be from head office to head office via written forms and never verbally.

To be clear, the NHL will set the guidelines and rules, the third party will dispense the justice and no more "wheel of justice" on suspensions or how games are officiated. There can't be anymore interpretations and guessing what was in a player's mind. The rules are set and that's that.

There should be female referees and linesman immediately. There's absolutely no reason whatsoever women can't do these jobs and they should do these jobs.

NHL COMMISSIONER

I think Gary Bettman has been a wizard at keeping the NHL afloat and profitable and growing. I also think he has never, nor the board of Governors, ever meant to throw the game into the doldrums. But the road to hell is always paved with good intentions. I think the commissioner needs to be beholden to no owners meaning Bettman should have absolute power for the good of the game.

There should be a rules committee that meets every five years and only every five years unless it's something the commissioner wishes to address right away. The rules committee should have only five owners who are randomly chosen every five years and the owners who own the league should make any rule changes which can be vetoed by the commissioner if he, or she, chooses.

The commissioner should be at arms-length from the GMs and the owners so that he or she is free to do whatever is best for the NHL without hesitation or blowback from angry owners.

DIVERSITY COMMITTEE

A committee should be setup right away to increase diversity in the NHL. Like the referees there are no female general managers or assistant coaches or coaches and there should be immediately. There should also be female presidents and vice-presidents.

It's not political correctness. It's just smart business - they make up 51 percent of the customer base - they need to be directing traffic to get the customer what he or she wants. They also bring a different perspective to any organization. And how many hockey mothers out there went to every single game their son or daughter played? Hundreds of thousands is the answer. It's not an exclusive male club.

The other diversity is the white factor. Indigenous peoples and African Canadian and Americans, Asians and East Indians are way underrepresented in the NHL. Find out what they need, and make it happen and if necessary mandate a draft rule that 10 percent of a team's draft is a visible minority. It's not a lot. It's one player every two years. But it's a start and it has to start somewhere. I abhor affirmative action but in this case it might be necessary.

Now this is not to in anyway suggest there is racism in the NHL at any level. I don't think for one second that a person's colour comes into drafting or hiring. What I'm referring to is getting pro-active and saying, hey, we're not diverse enough and it's hurting business and we've got to kick start this because money is waiting. It's an opportunity that's being lost.

It should be a priority to get into African American or African Canadian communities and ask what they need to get going in hockey. They may already do this to some extent but it should be given a higher priority. Get into First Nations towns and build rinks and really reach out to them even more than the NHL has done so. Get a committee together with former NHL First Nations players and the NHL and governments and start talking.

Sometimes it just starts with sitting down and saying, "Ok, how can I help?"

My idea would be to create a National First Nations Junior League. If they're not coming to us, then fine, we'll go to them. As a Canadian I wouldn't care one bit if this is something they need and want and will help them and they need some tax dollars to run the buses, I say, fine. Anytime we get into sports and not something else it's a win. Period.

REDUCING PARTICIPATION COST

The NHL is sharing revenue amongst its teams but it needs to help fund lower income children so they can get into hockey. One of the problems is a lack of facilities which drives minor hockey costs up. The NHL has to fund construction of at least two new arenas in a random municipality every year in both the US and Canada.

If the NHL wants to address its talent shortage it has to start building from the ground up. The payoff for the NHL is stars which leads to higher tv ratings which increases revenues. It's planting the crop. This is something the NFL, NBA and MLB don't have to do because every high-school in America has a field or basketball court. Hockey is different. It's a longterm fix to a longterm issue.

FAN EXPERIENCE

The commissioner must make more of an attempt to address scoring issues by first stating the obvious - the NHL has a scoring issue. He has to clearly outline the steps the NHL is going to take to give a better fan experience. And the NHLPA has to stand up for its customers as well and give the go-ahead for aggressive cuts to goalie equipment. It got way out of hand and if the NHL doesn't address the lack of goals per game it's going to be on the downward slope soon in revenues and that means downward slope in salary for the players. It's in everyone's best interest to make it a 5-4 league or as close as possible. Nine goals over a 60 minute game is not asking a lot.

Ticket prices are extreme in some cities. Obviously it's a free market system and so the market will determine the prices. However, it would be nice if there was a mandate from the NHL to work to providing a more affordable experience.

WINS LOSSES TIES

Go back to the simple formula that worked for years and years. Wins, loss and ties. Cut the game after 60 minutes and let everyone go home after a two hour game. Keep the fans' best interest at heart. And give the game back to the statistics keepers. The natural process of good teams at the top and the bad teams at the bottom needs to come back.

TROPHY CORRECTION

Balance out media participation. One vote per city. Do the same for the Hall of Fame, one vote per NHL city. It's not really a league if everyone comes from the same place. There is an award called the Lou Marsh Award which Toronto media self-proclaimed as Canada's "athlete of the year." Almost all of the voters are in Toronto. Most people outside of Toronto call the Canadian Press "Canada Athlete of the Year Award" the official award because it does a better job of including Canada. The NHL awards will only get better with full North American NHL participation.

UNIFORMS

Home whites and away dark uniforms for half the season and then switch to dark home jerseys and dark away uniforms for the other half. It gives fans an opportunity to see all the team's colours and avoid the same colour playing the same colour each and every night.

AMERICAN BROADCASTS

Oh for Pete's sake, please try a new crew. Change it up. Get a Canadian play-by-play caller who grew up with the game and get some stars on the broadcasts for the whole show, not just the intermissions.

HALL OF FAME

Let's have a discussion on where the Hall of Fame should be located and a real discussion on who gets in and how and start new. It's a Canadian conversation not a Toronto conversation. There are people and players in the HHOF who shouldn't be in there in most objective fans views. Scrub it, start new.

ILLEGAL DEFENSE

Open up the slot by eliminating the blocking of the "house" with five defenders standing in front of the net. Two men must be above the face-off circles at all times. Enforce "unsportsmanlike" conduct by calling people who fall on the ice to block a shot or call it what it is - unsportsmanlike conduct. This should eliminate five guys laying on the ice all the time in their own zone.

COACHES

Cap the maximum number of coaches per team at two. How teams divide it up is up to them. There's too many coaches right now and too many coaches means less offense.

BAN VIDEO REVIEW

Remove all electronic devices from the bench including coaches' headsets and ipads. No electronic devices permitted. Remove all coaches challenges and video reviews on anything, what the referee says stands. Reinstate the goal judge behind the net with her or his red light. It's not a science seminar it's a game played by humans, let it go.

WOODEN STICKS

No aluminum or graphite or carbon fibre sticks. Do you have any idea what these cost for parents? A stick is just a tool. There's zero evidence players shoot faster with these science contraptions than wooden sticks. Al MacInnis is still the gold standard in the NHL and he played with a wooden stick. And these carbon fibre sticks just break on impact anyways time and time again. That affects goal totals. Get rid of them. MLB just uses wooden bats. So did the NHL until manufacturers saw dollar signs in their eyes and went to the moon building $400 sticks. That's ridiculous. It's just a tool. A $20 stick works as well as a $400 stick. A pass is a pass - what matters is where it's headed. A shot is a shot - what matters is how it's done, not what it's done with. I've seen roofers with an old fashioned hammer beat someone using a nail gun in laying down a roof. They're fantastic to watch. Learn to use the tools of the trade. (Although roof guns are damned nice.) If you can't shoot the puck hard with a wooden stick you shouldn't be in the NHL.

FULL LENGTH GLOVES

It's a safety issue for kids. And again, if you have a hard time shooting the puck wearing proper hockey gloves then you shouldn't be in the NHL. And judging by the lack of goals in the NHL it hasn't exactly helped. It's a stupid thing and a safety concern that trickles down to the minor leagues. Ban the short gloves.

SMALLER SHOULDER PADS

There's no good reason for hard plastic shoulder pads or hard plastic elbow pads. I can't think of a single reason you would need these football pads in hockey. It should hurt the person throwing a hit a little bit and with softer old-fashioned pads - no one gets knocked unconscious, or at least are less likely too be knocked out.

SOFT PADDING ON OUTSIDE OF HELMETS

If you put the padding on the outside of the helmet, combined with a hard shell and padding on the inside it's going to lessen the blow if someone is hit to the head. It was a soft shell in football and rugby still has these types of helmets. It should be at least 1" thick and of very soft material. Allow someone to wear independent helmets inside the helmet and gloves inside the gloves so if they fight they have extra protection and so does the person they're fighting.

ORIGINAL SIX

Kill the stupid saying. Issue a memo from the head office to stop using it on air. It's offensive in many different ways and meant to be offensive i.e. we're better than you.

Commemorate and celebrate Vancouver and Los Angeles with heritage designations and put 110 year patch on the Canucks shirt.

Return the Lester Patrick Cup to Vancouver; open a west coast Hall of Fame in Vancouver and celebrate Vancouver's rich hockey history; hang their many championship banners.

This is a no-brainer. The NHL has allowed the west to feel like second class citizens. This is stupid for business. The Western Conference needs to know when they're hosting a Vancouver or a Los Angeles they're hosting really old hockey traditions just like Montreal or Toronto. They are clubs going back, in Vancouver's case, more than a century.

History is not something to be ashamed of, and in the case of the NHL, gloat over. Celebrate the competing league. Embrace its traditions. Sell more tickets and jerseys and put eyeballs on tv sets. It just makes good business sense. You can't have six teams in the East celebrated as special and nothing in the west, especially since it isn't true. Get neck deep in the Pacific Coast

Hockey Association. Put it right there with the NHL. And this means special attention from the national tv rights holders in both countries. Take it up a notch. Embrace the history of all of the teams. Extinguish the "six." Don't make games with team 25 verses team 27 feel like just a waste of time. Celebrate and embrace the uniqueness of all markets. Think big and stop being small.

NHL SUMMER BALL HOCKEY LEAGUE

My goodness this is another no-brainer. Pull the ice out of the NHL arenas at the end of May, sign up some kids, have tryouts, pay them $20,000 a summer, and crank up the music - broadcast the games. Put the emphasis on fun, let the music play for the whole game. Let the guys sit on the boards. Go eight on eight. Make the coaches play a shift. Have fun. Go nuts with it. Go outdoors in the parking lot for a game. Get in the sun. Get on the beach in the cities. Celebrate road hockey for what it is - terrific sport and exercise. Sponsor it. Broadcast it. Trade players. Have a Saturday night game of the week. Do it up.

This also ties in with the new Hockey leagues that emphasize hockey and play ball hockey.

I mean this is about as basic as it gets in business 101 - stay open all year. Who knows? A couple of the kids might even earn NHL tryouts. And at least half the NHL is open for summer business in May. And don't have the fans sitting in the stands. Get them walking around the game. Get other stuff going on in the stands. Maybe even play a simultaneous game of hurling or lacrosse. Get people standing, walking around, playing, faces on the glass.

1875 PATCH

Hockey is as old as baseball. In fact, the first major league baseball game was played in Canada. Celebrate the fact hockey has been around a very long time and make sure everyone in the USA knows it. Put the 1875 patch on the uniforms for a year.

USA HOCKEY

America is now producing the best players in the game - either from the NCAA or high-school ranks - the NHL needs to celebrate this turning of the page from Canada to the USA by putting an American flag on its logo or turning it red, white and blue. America needs to know it is the best at hockey now and that it is in fact an American game and the NHL should be supporting it. And Canadian hockey needs to follow their example as outlined previously. And for Canadians who are outraged - if it wasn't for the NY Rangers or Boston Bruins there would be no NHL so save your breath. And it was Seattle that moved the Stanley Cup to America.

DRAFT LOTTERY / THIRD PARTY

The lottery is weighted way too far to random. It needs to be returned to helping teams at the bottom of the standings. The team that gets the first overall pick is banned from getting another first overall pick for five years.

The entire lottery itself is turned over to the RCMP and/or FBI. I'm sure there isn't anything untoward going on right now, however, there are those with tinfoil hats who believe the Toronto Maple Leafs didn't win the lottery without help, nor the Edmonton Oilers etc. etc. And though the truth is the lottery is legitimate because it's held behind closed doors with a team paid for the by the NHL there is always going to be a conspiracy theory hanging over the NHL. Therefore it's better for the NHL to wash it's hands of it completely, turn it over to the authorities and say, "You do it."

SPEED

Do whatever is necessary to eliminate speed from the NHL because of injuries and because it favours kids who could pay for a lot of ice skating. It's not a pleasing sport when it's played the way it is today and with the problem of concussions, slowing the game down just makes sense. Parents will be more apt to put their kids in hockey if it includes ball hockey, affordable skating, and no head injuries. Think 30 years down the road.

INDIVIDUALITY
Help players "accessorize" on the ice. Have three or four different types of sweaters a player can wear, even with slightly different colours (but the same logo.) Some might want laces, some might want a V neck, some could have a tattered look, some might want squeaky clean. Get many different looking types of helmets with slightly different colours. Allow them to put stickers on them. Get different types of skates, different colours of skates and skate laces. The goal is to encourage personality to shine through. Kids love stickers. If they can buy NHL stickers to put on their helmets or stick to look like an NHL star, fantastic.

PLAYOFFS
Make the regular season meaningful and give President Trophy winners every possible advantage to get to the Finals.

ADVERTISEMENTS
Get the advertisements off the ice surface and never put them on sweaters.

SPEAK UP!
Former NHL players need to start criticizing the system. It's going to take more than Phil Esposito, Dan Boyle and Bobby Orr to stand up and say the game needs help. Former stars need to be heard. They need to get involved with the Canadian government and work to removing bureaucracy in Hockey Canada or whatever they feel needs to be done. When Orr says kids are

playing too many games then we need to listen and take action.

STRUCTURE REMOVAL
Under the age of 14 kids shouldn't be taught any systems other than some basic breakout plays. Practices should involve little to no coaching. Three on three hockey games in the three zones. And no goalies. The main objective is to score goals. Focus has to be fun and free form and no standing around not moving waiting for drills. There shouldn't be any coaching manual with drill suggestions. That has to go away.

GET OUT OF THE GYM
Every minute in the gym is a minute not playing hockey. The puck will travel faster than anyone can skate and that's physics and human physiology. No amount of weight lifting changes the laws of nature. It's a time thief.

COACHING LIMIT
Limit the number of coaches at the NHL to two. Limit the number of coaches below the age of 14 to one. And ban electronic uses of headphones and iPads.

BAN FALLING TO THE ICE
It's a bad idea anyways given the razors skaters wear and the hard puck that can remove teeth. It's unsportsmanlike in all respects.

NEWLY BUILT RINKS IN THE NHL MUST BE DIFFERENT
Every rink today looks the same and has the same ice surface. It's incredibly boring. MLB got away from this "cookie cutter" style of field to great affect. The NHL got away from this when they had it. Boston and Buffalo had different size ice surfaces (smaller.) The buildings all had different quirks to them from bad lighting to

steep seating. Brooklyn has a smaller fan surface and it's quirky. They need more of this. Go a little bigger in some places. Go smaller in others. GMs can build teams accordingly.

TOP 25 HOCKEY PLAYERS

1. Patrick Roy - Changed hockey. If I could start a team in any time in any era and I wanted to win - it's Roy above all else.

2. Mario Lemieux - Magnificent. What couldn't he do?

3. Pavel Bure - Changed hockey. First world class athlete in the NHL. Only player on this list who did it solo, no help required, thank you.

4. Wayne Gretzky - When you think hockey you think Gretzky. But couldn't put him first because he never won without the gang.

5. Mike Bossy - Best pure sniper on planet Earth.

6. Nels Stewart - Held NHL scoring record for 25 years. If you computed a regular season of 82 games for him - 700 goals and 2000 pims. Two time Hart Trophy winner.

7. Bobby Orr - six stunning years.

8. Maurice Richard - 50 goals in 50 games, 8 Stanley Cups.

9. Jaromir Jagr - second all time goals is hard to deny.

10. Marcel Dionne - a ridiculous amount of goals playing a long, long ways from the NHL's eastern time zone all by himself.

11. Scott Neidermeyer - Capable of carrying an entire team by himself. Won everything, ever.

12. Guy Lafleur - More than the leader of the best dynasty in hockey history he gave hockey its beauty.

13. Mark Messier - Competitor who had the whole nine yards. Tarnished his career by staying a tad too long, otherwise would have been higher.

14. Cyclone Taylor - Champion. For six years averaged more than a goal per game. (Plus Cyclone - Are you going to argue with that?)

15. Gordie Howe - Consistency, 6 Art Ross Trophies; held scoring record in NHL from 1962 until Wayne Gretzky.

16. Howie Morenz - three time Hart Trophy winner, 3 Cups. Died from hockey.

17. Doug Harvey - Changed the PP rule because he was so dominant.

18. Alexander Ovechkin - Brute force from a giant of a man. May own the NHL scoring record when he leaves.

19. Phil Esposito - 77 goals. 1972. Enough said. (Go look again at his stats)

20. Brett Hull - The release. The shot.

21. Bobby Hull - 54 goals in 65 games; his consistency was ridiculous.

22. Jari Kurri - Was there anything scarier than Gretzky and Kurri coming down the ice? No. Not ever.

23. Nik Lidstrom - Had the advantage of a payroll team, otherwise would be higher.

24. Brian Leetch - Simply superb in every aspect of the game.

25. Duncan Keith - Is as close to Pavel Bure in a defenseman as we'll ever see.

26. Sidney Crosby - He would have been higher except for the unbalanced schedule.

27. Joe Sakic - The most forgotten and underrated hockey player of all time.

28. Eddie Shore - Hockey.

29. Ron Francis - smooth as butter.

30. Bryan Trottier - 4 time Cup winner. Any place, any time, any where.

31. Larry Robinson. - Big Bird. 6 Cups as a player, 4 as a coach.

CREDITS

Statista.com - NHL revenue source
https://www.statista.com/statistics/193468/total-league-revenue-of-the-nhl-since-2006/

Dan Rosen
NHL.com
A general breakdown of just some of the rule changes over the past decade.

Washington Post, June 1, 2016
Julianna Miner
"Why 70 percent of kids quit sport by age 13"
https://www.washingtonpost.com/news/parenting/wp/2016/06/01/why-70-percent-of-kids-quit-sports-by-age-13/?utm_term=.349ca462ab8a

USA Hockey website
http://www.admkids.com/about
What are the Benefits of Hosting a Major League Sports Franchise?
By Jordan Rappaport and Chad Wilkerson
Jordan Rappaport is an economist at the Federal Reserve Bank of Kansas City. Chad Wilkerson is an associate economist at the bank. This article is on the bank's web site at www.kc.frb.org

Adam Silver, NBA commissioner, talking about expansion in a CBS article with Matt Moore talks about each team having a requirement for all 30 teams in the NBA being "must-see" experiences.

John Ferguson, the Montreal Canadiens great from Vancouver who played lacrosse in Nanaimo. This is his bio from wikipedia.

PHOTO CREDIT

Port McNeill Junior Braves photo, by Michael Munro
Air Force goalie, by Skeeze
Dead Puck Era, graphic by Michael Munro, tombstone
graphic Alexas_Fotos
Soccer playing, Keith Johnston, KeithJJ Pixabay.
Referee Jumping in Air, Keith Johnston, KeithJJ,
Pixabay
Money, Kelvin Stuttard
Airplane, Achim Thiemermann

ABOUT THE AUTHOR

Michael Munro is a graduate of the 1992 Langara University (then known as Vancouver Community College, Langara Campus) Journalism program. He went on to study English Literature at British Columbia Open University (which is now known as Thompson River University).

Prior to that he made brief and somewhat lucid stops at Capilano College (now known as Capilano University) where he studied something including philosophy and Malaspina University (now known as Vancouver Island University) where he remembers a business course.

Somewhere between then and there he worked for some community newspapers in Vancouver and Nanaimo covering everything from the Vancouver Canucks (Pat Quinn era) to general beat and court reporting and the political scene having interviewed three British Columbia premiers and watched all three get booted out of office. Not due to any of his work but because this is British Columbia, home of the wild wild west. He was once fired from a newspaper for writing a column about leveling a neighbouring community and turning it into a golf course (story to come). He is currently and surprisingly employed.

Michael grew up on the Queen Charlotte Islands (now known as Haida Gwaii) and moved to North Vancouver Island then regressed in Vancouver and Nanaimo while his hair grayed. The community is currently considering changing its name.